Teach ★ Terrific GRAMMAR

For Grades 6–8

Gary Robert Muschla

New York   Chicago   San Francisco   Lisbon   London   Madrid   Mexico City
Milan   New Delhi   San Juan   Seoul   Singapore   Sydney   Toronto

1 2 3 4 5 6 7 8 9 10 11 12 13 14 15 16 17 18 19 20 21 22 23 24 25 QPD/QPD 0 9 8 7 6

ISBN-13: 978-0-07-147703-1
ISBN-10:   0-07-147703-9

Library of Congress Control Number: 2006925753

Interior design by Nick Panos

McGraw-Hill books are available at special quantity discounts to use as premiums and sales promotions, or for use in corporate training programs. For more information, please write to the Director of Special Sales, Professional Publishing, McGraw-Hill, Two Penn Plaza, New York, NY 10121-2298. Or contact your local bookstore.

This book is printed on acid-free paper.

Contents

Part 2   Nouns **27**

Part 3   Verbs **47**

About This Book

Most students find the rules of English grammar to be confusing, if not outright overwhelming. Adding to the muddle are the many exceptions to the rules that are just plain maddening. But understanding grammar is essential for students to speak and write with competence and clarity.

Teach Terrific Grammar, Grades 6–8 can be a valuable resource in teaching grammar to your students. Reproducible tip sheets throughout the book highlight important grammatical facts and rules, and self-correcting reproducible worksheets provide students with an interesting way to learn and practice grammar skills.

Teaching grammar can be challenging. Learning grammar can be even more challenging. It is my hope that this book will make the study of grammar in your classroom an enjoyable and successful experience for both you and your students.

How to Use This Book

Teach *Terrific Grammar, Grades 6–8* is divided into nine parts, each of which concentrates on grammar skills and includes reproducible tip sheets and worksheets. An answer key for the worksheets is included at the end of the book.

Part 1 "Sentences" includes three tips sheets and seventeen worksheets that focus on sentence types, sentence structure, subjects, predicates, fragments, and run-on sentences. In addition, four review worksheets are included at the end of this section.

Part 2 "Nouns" includes four tip sheets and ten worksheets that focus on singular nouns, plural nouns, common nouns, proper nouns, irregular plural nouns, and possessive nouns. The section concludes with four review worksheets.

Part 3 "Verbs" contains six tip sheets and twenty-nine worksheets that cover action verbs, linking verbs, verb phrases, direct objects, indirect objects, predicate nominatives, predicate adjectives, contractions with verbs, tenses, irregular verbs, and subject-verb agreement. Three review worksheets conclude this section of the book.

Part 4 "Pronouns" contains five tip sheets and sixteen worksheets on personal pronouns, antecedents, subject pronouns, object pronouns, possessive pronouns, and indefinite pronouns. Three review worksheets are also included.

Part 5 "Adjectives" contains two tip sheets and seven worksheets on identifying adjectives and proper adjectives and the comparison of adjectives. Three review worksheets conclude this section.

Part 6 "Adverbs" includes three tip sheets and eight worksheets on identifying adverbs, the comparison of adverbs, and double negatives. The section also includes three review worksheets.

Part 7 "Prepositions, Conjunctions, and Interjections" contains four tip sheets and ten worksheets on prepositions, prepositional phrases, adjective phrases, adverb phrases, conjunctions, and interjections. The section ends with four review worksheets.

Part 8 "Punctuation and Capitalization" contains eight tip sheets and twenty-three worksheets on end punctuation, commas, colons, semicolons, apostrophes, quotation marks, italics, and capitalization. Eleven review worksheets are also included.

Part 9 "Usage and Proofreading" contains one tip sheet and six worksheets on words that cause confusion, and one tip sheet and eight worksheets on proofreading to find grammatical mistakes.

The tip sheets and worksheets throughout the book are designed to make your teaching easier and more effective. Both tip sheets and worksheets can stand alone and be used with students of varying abilities. Each tip sheet serves as a resource, providing facts and information about topics and skills in grammar, and can be used to introduce, review, or clarify material. Like the tip sheets, you may use the worksheets in a variety of ways: for supplementing your instruction in grammar, for reinforcement, for extra credit, for challenges, or for substitute plans.

The reproducible worksheets are designed for easy implementation. The worksheets have clear directions and require no additional materials, although you may want to encourage your students to consult the appropriate tip sheet or their language arts book if they need help in completing the worksheets. Moreover, the worksheets are self-correcting. Students are presented with a trivia question at the top of the worksheet, which they can answer by completing the worksheet correctly. The questions that begin the worksheets are derived from various subjects, including literature, geography, history, science, and pop culture.

The skills covered in this book follow the typical language arts and grammar curriculum for grades 6 through 8. The skill or topic addressed in each worksheet is included with the number and title of the worksheet in the Contents. The Contents therefore serves as a skills list, making it easy for you to identify the reproducibles that will be of most benefit to your students.

As you go through the contents, you will find that some skills and topics are addressed by two, three, or more worksheets. In such cases, the worksheets progress in difficulty from basic to more challenging, the first worksheet of the set being designated by 1, the second by 2, the third by 3, and so on.

The reproducible tip sheets and worksheets throughout this book offer 206 separate activities for your students. They will provide your students with a variety of activities that will help them to gain a greater understanding of grammar.

Sentences

A sentence, in its simplest form and structure, is an arrangement of words that expresses a complete thought. Sentences are the foundation of communication in English.

The tip sheets and worksheets contained in this section focus on sentences. The first tip sheet and Worksheets 1.1 through 1.3 focus on sentence types and structure. The second tip sheet and Worksheets 1.4 through 1.14 concentrate on subjects and predicates. The third tip sheet and Worksheets 1.15 through 1.17 concentrate on fragments and run-on sentences, and Worksheets 1.18 through 1.21 provide reviews of sentences.

Kinds and Structures of Sentences

Sentences may be one of four kinds:

1. A *declarative* sentence makes a statement. It ends with a period:

   The rain ruined the picnic.

2. An *interrogative* sentence asks a question. It ends with a question mark:

   Do you have homework tonight?

3. An *imperative* sentence gives a command or makes a request. It ends with a period:

   Please open the window.

4. An *exclamatory* sentence expresses strong emotion. It ends with an exclamation point:

   Look out for the car!

Sentences may also be classified according to structure:

- A *simple* sentence has one complete subject and one complete predicate:

  Tom went to band practice.

- A *compound* sentence contains two or more simple sentences that may be joined by a conjunction such as *and, but, or,* or *nor.* A comma usually comes before the conjunction. Sometimes a semicolon may join the simple sentences. The simple sentences that make up a compound sentence are called *independent,* or *main,* clauses:

  Terri came home from school, and she started her homework.

- A *complex* sentence contains one independent clause and at least one *dependent,* or *subordinate,* clause. The independent clause can stand alone. The dependent clause cannot:

  When the alarm went off, Danny automatically hit the snooze button.

1.1 Lost Voyage

In 1872 a ship left New York for Genoa, Italy. Four weeks later the ship was found afloat in the Atlantic Ocean with all of its sails set. There was no sign of any tragedy, but the crew was gone. What was the name of this ill-fated ship?

To answer the question, identify each sentence below as declarative, interrogative, imperative, or exclamatory. Write the letter of each answer in the space above its sentence number at the bottom of the page.

1. People have been sailing the seas for thousands of years.
   L. Declarative   R. Interrogative   M. Imperative   D. Exclamatory

2. What time does your ship leave port?
   A. Declarative   S. Interrogative   N. Imperative   W. Exclamatory

3. One of the worst shipping disasters of all time was the sinking of the *Titanic*.
   R. Declarative   O. Interrogative   A. Imperative   T. Exclamatory

4. Please open the window.
   T. Declarative   I. Interrogative   C. Imperative   S. Exclamatory

5. Is the captain an experienced seaman?
   E. Declarative   Y. Interrogative   U. Imperative   H. Exclamatory

6. Ask that crewman for directions.
   L. Declarative   H. Interrogative   A. Imperative   I. Exclamatory

7. Look out for that big wave!
   E. Declarative   S. Interrogative   U. Imperative   T. Exclamatory

8. What time is dinner?
   K. Declarative   E. Interrogative   N. Imperative   D. Exclamatory

9. I wonder whether a storm is coming.
   M. Declarative   A. Interrogative   J. Imperative   S. Exclamatory

___ ___ ___ ___   ___ ___ ___ ___ ___ ___ ___
 9   6   3   5   4   8   1   8   2   7   8

1.2 Mystery Author

This writer is known for his haunting poetry and chilling stories. He is considered to be the father of the modern mystery. Who is he?

To answer the question, identify the structure of each sentence below. Select your answers from the choices after each sentence. Write the letter of each answer in the space above its sentence number at the bottom of the page. You will need to divide the letters into words.

1. James enjoys horror stories, but he likes mysteries more.
   R. Simple   N. Compound

2. People have been telling stories for thousands of years.
   D. Simple   A. Compound

3. Stephen King, master of the horror story, is one of Sara's favorite authors.
   O. Simple   E. Compound

4. Although scary movies give Marcia nightmares, she loves watching them.
   T. Compound   R. Complex

5. On Saturday Melissa went to the bookstore, and she bought several novels.
   E. Compound   C. Complex

6. Whenever Vincent goes to the mall, he stops at the bookstore.
   W. Compound   G. Complex

7. During the snowstorm, Taylor read *The Outsiders* by S. E. Hinton.
   P. Simple   H. Complex

8. Lindsay could read a mystery for her book report, or she could read a romance.
   L. Compound   U. Complex

9. Steve reads fantasy novels because he likes reading about brave heroes, powerful villains, and magic.
   T. Simple   A. Complex

___ ___ ___ ___ ___ ___ ___ ___ ___ ___ ___ ___ ___
 5   2   6   9   4   9   8   8   9   1   7   3   5

1.3 Worthy of a Great King

According to legend, Britain's King Arthur possessed a magical, unbreakable sword. What was the name of this sword?

To answer the question, identify the structure of each sentence below. Write the letter of each answer in the space above its sentence number at the bottom of the page.

1. Although much legend surrounds King Arthur, most historians believe he was a real man.

   I. Simple   E. Compound   U. Complex

2. An ancient Briton king by the name of Arthur lived around 500 A.D.

   A. Simple   K. Compound   D. Complex

3. According to legend, Arthur pulled a sword from a stone, and he became king.

   T. Simple   I. Compound   M. Complex

4. Arthur's chief advisor was Merlin, a wizard.

   C. Simple   R. Compound   H. Complex

5. When he was king of the Britons, Arthur led a war against invading armies.

   E. Simple   N. Compound   B. Complex

6. Guinevere was Arthur's beautiful queen, and Sir Lancelot was his friend.

   T. Simple   E. Compound   I. Complex

7. Arthur's court was at the magnificent castle of Camelot.

   L. Simple   W. Compound   K. Complex

8. Mordred was Arthur's nephew, but Mordred betrayed Arthur.

   N. Simple   R. Compound   D. Complex

9. When Arthur fell in his final battle, legend says he was carried away to the island of Avalon to be healed.

   H. Simple   U. Compound   X. Complex

___ ___ ___ ___ ___ ___ ___ ___ ___
 6   9   4   2   7   3   5   1   8

Subjects and Predicates

Sentences are built around subjects and predicates. In the following examples the subjects and predicates are italicized.

- The *complete subject* of a sentence includes all the words that tell who or what the sentence is about:

  James is an excellent baseball player.

  The powerful storm swept up the coast.

  The snow will fall throughout the night.

- The *simple subject* is the most important word or words in the complete subject. The simple subject is usually a noun or pronoun:

  James is an excellent baseball player.

  The powerful *storm* swept up the coast.

  The *snow* will fall throughout the night.

- Subjects may be compound. A *compound subject* has two or more simple subjects:

  Roberto and *Anna* are twins.

- The *complete predicate* of a sentence includes all the words that tell what the subject is or does:

  James *is an excellent baseball player.*

  The powerful storm *swept up the coast.*

  The snow *will fall throughout the night.*

- The *simple predicate* is the most important word or words in the complete predicate. It is a verb or a verb phrase:

  James *is* an excellent baseball player.

  The powerful storm *swept* up the coast.

  The snow *will fall* throughout the night.

- A predicate may be compound, which means it has two or more simple predicates:

  Jason *swims* and *jogs* for exercise.

Name _____ Date _____

1.4 Famous Lady

Leonardo da Vinci was a scientist, inventor, musician, and painter. One of his most famous paintings was of a woman. What painting was this?

To answer the question, identify the complete subject and complete predicate of each sentence below. Find the letter beneath the slash that divides the sentence into a complete subject and complete predicate. Then write the letter above its sentence number at the bottom of the page. You will need to divide the letters into words.

1. Leonardo da / Vinci / was born / in Italy / in 1452.
           A   O   S   L

2. He / received / an / excellent / education.
   L   M   R   H

3. In school / Leonardo / studied / reading, writing, / and mathematics.
       E   H   R   I

4. The / boy / excelled at / music, painting, / and mechanical devices.
    E   S   I   R

5. As / a young man, / Leonardo / became interested / in many subjects.
    L   P   N   D

6. Leonardo / filled notebooks / with his / observations / and ideas.
        T   R   C   M

7. With much care / he / based / his ideas / on observation.
          D M   S   W

8. Five hundred / years / ago / the inventor / drew plans for an airplane.
        U   N   E   A

9. Leonardo / was also / one of the first / painters / to draw realistic landscapes.
      I   G   L   C

10. He / will / be remembered as / one of the most / brilliant men of all time.
   E   U   I   Y

___ ___ ___ ___ ___ ___ ___ ___ ___ ___ ___
6   3   10   7   1   5   8   2   9   4   8

Sentences

© Gary Robert Muschla

7

Sentences

1.5 Greatest Cowboy

Pecos Bill is an American folk hero. Although many people know about Bill's adventures in the Old West, not many know about his wife. Who was Pecos Bill's wife?

To answer the question, decide whether the slash divides each sentence into its complete subject and complete predicate. If the sentence is divided correctly, write the letter for "correct" in the space above its sentence number at the bottom of the page. If the sentence is divided incorrectly, write the letter for "incorrect." You will need to divide the letters into words.

1. According to folklore, Pecos Bill / was born in Texas in the 1830s.
   U. Correct   E. Incorrect

2. Bill was the greatest cowboy / who ever lived.
   M. Correct   T. Incorrect

3. As a baby, / Bill used a big knife as a teething ring.
   H. Correct   O. Incorrect

4. In some stories Bill was raised / by coyotes.
   N. Correct   E. Incorrect

5. No problem / was too big for Bill.
   L. Correct   H. Incorrect

6. Bill rode / a mountain lion for fun.
   K. Correct   U. Incorrect

7. He / used a rattlesnake for a whip.
   E. Correct   L. Incorrect

8. His horse's / name was Widow-Maker.
   M. Correct   F. Incorrect

9. Bill was famous / for many great feats.
   S. Correct   O. Incorrect

10. During a drought he / lassoed a tornado to bring rain.
    S. Correct   D. Incorrect

11. Pecos Bill / became a symbol for the American frontier.
    S. Correct   M. Incorrect

___ ___ ___ ___   -   ___ ___ ___ ___ ___ ___ ___
10   5   1   7   8   3   9   2   11 6   4

1.6 Sense or Nonsense

Lewis Carroll is the author of a poem that at first seems to be nonsense. But with a closer reading and a little imagination the poem begins to make sense. What is the name of this poem?

To answer the question, find the simple subject in each of the sentences below. Choose your answers from among the underlined words. Write the letter beneath the simple subject in the space above its sentence number at the bottom of the page.

1. Lewis Carroll's real name was Charles Lutwidge Dodgson.
   A   O M   C

2. Carroll was an author and a mathematician.
   R H   D   N

3. The man was born in England in 1832.
   A I E   L

4. After graduating from college, Carroll became a mathematician.
   S J   T   C

5. He is best known for the story *Alice's Adventures in Wonderland.*
   E U   H   J

6. The character of Alice was based on Alice Liddell, a young girl.
   K   H   E   I

7. Carroll went on to write several books for children.
   Y   D   N   S

8. Do you know the titles of some of those books?
   B   L F   R

9. His delightful fantasy appeals to both children and adults.
   S J W   V

10. The stories of Lewis Carroll are known throughout the world.
    J   B   O   D

___ ___ ___ ___ ___ ___ ___ ___ ___ ___ ___
10 3   8   8   5   2   9   1   4   6   7

1.7 Not-So-Famous Horse

On the night of April 18, 1775, Paul Revere began his ride from Boston to Concord to warn the patriots that British troops were coming. Most people know the name of Paul Revere. But what was the name of his horse?

To answer the question, read the article below and identify the simple subject of each sentence. Starting with the first simple subject, write the letters beneath the simple subjects in order on the blanks at the bottom of the page. You will need to divide the letters into words.

Are <u>you</u> familiar with the <u>midnight</u> ride of Paul Revere? <u>Paul Revere</u> was born in
     B   T   R

<u>Boston</u> in 1735. A silversmith and engraver by <u>trade</u>, <u>he</u> was a steadfast <u>patriot</u>. With
  D   N O   J

other <u>patriots</u>, <u>Revere</u> took part in the <u>Boston Tea Party</u> of 1773. During the <u>war</u>, <u>Revere</u>
     K   W   H   C N

carried <u>messages</u> for patriot troops. With two other <u>men</u>, <u>he</u> carried his most important
     L   U B

message on the <u>night</u> of April 18, 1775. <u>He</u> hoped to warn the <u>patriots</u> of approaching
       S   E   V

British troops. In a strange <u>twist</u> of history that night, <u>Revere</u> did not warn the patriots.
                H   A

British <u>scouts</u> stopped and questioned him. Fortunately, <u>one</u> of the other men with
     U   T

<u>Revere</u> was able to slip by the British scouts and warn the patriots. A <u>poem</u>, "Paul
  W   Y

Revere's Ride," by Henry Wadsworth Longfellow, secured a place in history for <u>Revere</u>.
                                  A

__ __ __ __ __ __ __ __ __ __ __ __

1.8 First English Child of the New World

In 1587, Virginia Dare was the first English child born in America. Where was she born?

To answer the question, find the simple predicate in each of the sentences below. Choose your answers from among the underlined words. Write the letter beneath the simple predicate in the space above its sentence number at the bottom of the page. You will need to divide the letters into words.

1. A <u>voyage</u> from <u>Europe</u> to the <u>New World</u> <u>took</u> several weeks.
    M   D   R   K

2. The <u>long</u> <u>trip</u> <u>required</u> <u>courage</u> and strength.
     S   L   E   J

3. Upon <u>arrival</u>, the <u>colonists'</u> hard <u>work</u> <u>began</u>.
      N   Y   C   S

4. <u>Life</u> <u>was</u> <u>difficult</u> in the new <u>colony</u>.
  U   N   E   C

5. <u>Land</u> <u>must be cleared</u> for <u>the</u> <u>planting</u> of crops.
    H   I   V   M

6. <u>Everyone</u> <u>worked</u> together <u>in</u> order to <u>survive</u>.
    P   R   K   O

7. Disease, starvation, and <u>hostile</u> Native <u>Americans</u> <u>were</u> constant <u>threats</u>.
                     Y   U   A   M

8. Slowly <u>settlements</u> <u>were carved</u> <u>out</u> of the wilderness.
       M   L   W   G

9. Several <u>European</u> colonies <u>were started</u> in the <u>Americas</u>.
       M   T   D   I

10. In time the <u>colonies</u> <u>sought</u> their <u>independence</u> from the <u>Old World</u>.
        U   O   N   R

$$\overline{\quad}\ \ \overline{\quad}\ \ \overline{\quad}\ \ \overline{\quad}\ \ \overline{\quad}\ \ \overline{\quad}\ \ \overline{\quad}\ \ \overline{\quad}\ \ \overline{\quad}\ \ \overline{\quad}\ \ \overline{\quad}\ \ \overline{\quad}\ \ \overline{\quad}$$
  6   10   7   4   10   1   2   5   3   8   7   4   9

1.9 Batter Up!

The city of Cincinnati was the home of the first professional baseball team. What was the team's name?

   To answer the question, read the article below and identify the simple predicate of each sentence. Starting with the first simple predicate, write the letters beneath the simple predicates in order on the blanks at the bottom of the page. You will need to divide the letters into words.

Baseball <u>is</u> an American <u>game</u>. Early versions <u>of the game</u> <u>were based</u> on the
     R   B   U   E

British games of cricket and rounders. Both cricket and rounders <u>are played</u> with <u>teams</u>
                                                      D   C

and bats and a ball. In both games, players <u>score</u> points by <u>passing</u> stations, or bases.
                                      S   C

By the 1840s, American baseball <u>slowly</u> <u>was taking</u> its modern form. The game <u>grew</u> in
                                U   T   O

popularity <u>during</u> the 1850s. By the late 1850s several clubs <u>played</u> the game. The first
          N   C

<u>professional</u> baseball team <u>was started</u> in Cincinnati in 1869. Two years later, the first
     E   K

professional baseball <u>association</u> <u>was organized</u>. The National League, <u>still in operation</u>
                          D   I   M

today, <u>was founded</u> in 1876. Several other associations and leagues <u>followed</u>. <u>Teams</u> in
        N   G   H

the American League <u>began playing</u> in 1900. Because of its great popularity, baseball
                           S

<u>has been</u> called the national pastime.
     D

___ ___ ___ ___ ___ ___ ___ ___ ___ ___ ___ ___ ___ ___

1.10 Flying Disc

Most people know that a Frisbee is a toy flying disc that they can toss to their friends. Most people do not know that before they were called Frisbees, these flying discs had two other names. What was the second name for the Frisbee?

To answer the question, find the simple subject and simple predicate of each sentence below. Match your answers against the answers that are given for the sentence. Only *one* given answer—either the simple subject *or* the simple predicate—for each sentence is correct. Write the letter that follows each correct answer in the space above its sentence number at the bottom of the page. You will need to divide the letters into words.

1. Walter Frederick Morrison invented a flying disc in 1948.
   Subject: flying disc, M   Predicate: invented, O

2. Morrison called his flying disc the "Flying Saucer."
   Subject: Morrison, E   Predicate: flying, I

3. The original flying disc was not very popular.
   Subject: original, T   Predicate: was, R

4. The inventor worked on improving his flying disc.
   Subject: flying disc, A   Predicate: worked, U

5. He decided to give his invention another name.
   Subject: He, A   Predicate: give, M

6. In 1957 the Wham-O company bought Morrison's flying toy.
   Subject: flying toy, W   Predicate: bought, L

7. Wham-O changed the name of the toy to Frisbee.
   Subject: Wham-O, S   Predicate: name, N

8. You can play many games with a Frisbee.
   Subject: games, R   Predicate: can play, P

9. Over the years countless people have enjoyed Frisbees.
   Subject: people, T   Predicate: enjoyed, G

___ ___ ___ ___ ___ ___ ___ ___ ___ ___ ___ ___ ___
 8   6   4   9   1   8   6   5   9   9   2   3   7

1.11 Comics

Sentences

The first comic book that was sold on newsstands in America was published in 1934. What was its name?

To answer the question, find the simple subject and simple predicate of each sentence below. Match your answers against the answers that are given for the sentence. Only *one* given answer—either the simple subject *or* the simple predicate—for each sentence is correct. Write the letter that follows each correct answer in the space above its sentence number at the bottom of the page. You will need to divide the letters into words.

1. The first American comic strips appeared in the 1890s.
   Subject: American, N   Predicate: appeared, S

2. These early comics were published in newspapers.
   Subject: comics, I   Predicate: were, D

3. Soon newspapers around the country contained comic strips.
   Subject: country, D   Predicate: contained, A

4. Countless readers enjoyed the comics.
   Subject: readers, U   Predicate: comics, M

5. The themes of many early comic strips were based on life.
   Subject: themes, O   Predicate: based, T

6. By the 1930s, several different kinds of comics had appeared.
   Subject: comics, I   Predicate: had appeared, E

7. Adventure stories quickly became popular.
   Subject: stories, F   Predicate: quickly, R

8. The modern comic book was created in the 1930s.
   Subject: modern, T   Predicate: was created, N

9. People throughout the country read the comics each day.
   Subject: country, Y   Predicate: read, M

__	__	__	__	__	__	__	__	__	__	__	__	__
7	3	9	5	4	1	7	4	8	8	2	6	1

1.12 Holiday Report

Kim and her group were doing a report on holidays. They found that Memorial Day originally had a different name. What was Memorial Day originally called?

To answer the question, decide whether a compound subject is correctly underlined in each sentence below. If the compound subject is correctly identified, write the letter for "correct" in the space above its sentence number at the bottom of the page. If the compound subject is incorrectly identified, write the letter for "incorrect." You will need to divide the letters into words.

1. Kim and her group discussed which holidays to research.
   S. Correct   N. Incorrect

2. The Internet and books would likely provide plenty of information.
   E. Correct   A. Incorrect

3. Jason and Anna, two computer whizzes, searched the Internet.
   T. Correct   R. Incorrect

4. Computers and technology enabled the students to find information.
   T. Correct   M. Incorrect

5. Too many websites and too much information became a problem.
   C. Correct   U. Incorrect

6. Mrs. Williams, the school librarian, and the students checked sources together.
   O. Correct   M. Incorrect

7. Kim, Maria, and Justin found much of the same information.
   O. Correct   I. Incorrect

8. The beginnings and development of many holidays and celebrations can be traced far back in history.
   E. Correct   A. Incorrect

9. Written reports and oral presentations were part of the assignment.
   D. Correct   Y. Incorrect

10. Kim and Maria will present the oral part of the group's report.
    D. Correct   T. Incorrect

___ ___ ___ ___ ___ ___ ___ ___ ___ ___ ___ ___
10   2   5   6   3   8   4   7   6   1   10   8   9

1.13 Volleyball

Volleyball was invented in 1895. Who invented it?

To answer the question, decide whether a compound predicate is correctly underlined in each sentence below. If the compound predicate is correctly identified, write the letter for "correct" in the space above its sentence number at the bottom of the page. If the compound predicate is incorrectly identified, write the letter for "incorrect." You will need to divide the letters into words.

1. People around the world play and enjoy volleyball.
   R. Correct   T. Incorrect

2. Volleyball is a demanding game and requires great stamina.
   O. Correct   D. Incorrect

3. The standard court is sixty feet long and is divided by a net.
   S. Correct   G. Incorrect

4. A volleyball is about twenty-five inches around and weighs about ten ounces.
   N. Correct   E. Incorrect

5. The server hits the ball over the net and starts the game.
   W. Correct   M. Incorrect

6. The other team hits the ball and returns it over the net.
   U. Correct   A. Incorrect

7. Players may not catch, hold, or carry the ball.
   S. Correct   M. Incorrect

8. The ball must be returned within three hits and not be hit by the same player twice in succession.
   T. Correct   L. Incorrect

9. To score points, players jump and spike the ball over the net.
   I. Correct   O. Incorrect

__	__	__	__	__	__	__	__	__	__	__	__	__
5	9	8	8	9	6	7	7	2	1	3	6	4

1.14 Lightning Rod

In 1752, this man invented the lightning rod. A brilliant writer, statesman, and inventor, what was his name?

To answer the question, identify compound subjects and compound predicates in the sentences below. Match your answers against the answers that are given for the sentence. Only *one* given answer—either a compound subject (CS) *or* a compound predicate (CP)—for each sentence is correct. Write the letter that follows each correct answer in the space above its sentence number at the bottom of the page. You will need to divide the letters into words.

1. Lightning and thunder often occur in violent storms.
   CS: Lightning, thunder, A   CP: often, occur, U

2. Lightning is electricity and should be considered dangerous.
   CS: Lightning, electricity, C   CP: is, should be considered, K

3. The typical lightning bolt is about an inch wide and may be miles long.
   CS: lightning, bolt, E   CP: is, may be, I

4. Droplets of water and icy crystals rise and fall on air currents in clouds.
   CS: water, crystals, H   CP: rise, fall, R

5. The droplets and crystals collide and build up electrical charges.
   CS: droplets, crystals, E   CP: build up, O

6. Water droplets with positive charges rise and collect at the top of a cloud.
   CS: water, droplets, P   CP: rise, collect, L

7. Ice crystals with negative charges fall and gather at the base of a cloud.
   CS: crystals, charges, S   CP: fall, gather, F

8. Opposite charges attract and balance each other.
   CS: Opposite, charges, T   CP: attract, balance, B

9. The clap and rumble of thunder follow a flash of lightning.
   CS: clap, rumble, N   CP: follow, flash, M

___ ___ ___ ___ ___ ___ ___ ___ ___ ___ ___
 8   5   9   7   4   1   9   2   6   3   9

© Gary Robert Muschla

Sentences

Fragments and Run-On Sentences

Sentence fragments and run-on sentences are incorrect sentences.

- A *fragment* is a group of words that make up only part of a sentence. A fragment does not express a complete thought. A fragment may be missing a subject, a predicate, or both:

  A package to Louis.

  Finished her homework.

  The playful puppy.

- To correct a fragment, rewrite it so that it contains a subject and predicate:

  I sent a package to Louis.

  Kim finished her homework.

  The playful puppy bounded after the squeaky toy.

- A *run-on sentence* occurs when two or more separate sentences are joined incorrectly:

  The boys played video games they watched a movie.

  The magician was excellent, the audience marveled at his tricks.

- To correct a run-on, combine the ideas, or write the sentence as a compound sentence with the correct punctuation. You may also separate the different ideas and write them as two sentences:

  The boys played video games and watched a movie.

  The boys played video games, and they watched a movie.

  The boys played video games. They watched a movie.

  The magician was excellent, and the audience marveled at his tricks.

  The magician was excellent. The audience marveled at his tricks.

1.15 Lady Liberty

The Statue of Liberty, a symbol of freedom, stands at the entrance to New York Harbor. A sonnet written by Emma Lazarus is on its pedestal. What is the title of this sonnet?

   To answer the question, decide whether each example below is a complete sentence or a sentence fragment. Write the letter of each answer in the space above the example's number at the bottom of the page. You will need to divide the letters into words.

1. The Statue of Liberty was a gift from the French people.
   W. Complete sentence   R. Fragment

2. A proud woman in flowing robes and wearing a spiked crown, holding a torch.
   T. Complete sentence   L. Fragment

3. One of the largest statues in the world.
   R. Complete sentence   N. Fragment

4. Standing on Liberty Island and welcoming people to the United States.
   M. Complete sentence   C. Fragment

5. From the bottom of the pedestal to the tip of the torch, the statue is 305 feet high.
   E. Complete sentence   I. Fragment

6. Many immigrants saw the statue and wept with happiness.
   U. Complete sentence   E. Fragment

7. As they entered New York Harbor in search of a new life.
   U. Complete sentence   H. Fragment

8. People around the world look on the statue as a symbol of freedom.
   O. Complete sentence   I. Fragment

9. A national monument and tourist attraction today.
   C. Complete sentence   T. Fragment

10. The Statue of Liberty has given hope to millions of people.
   S. Complete sentence   N. Fragment

___ ___ ___ ___ ___ ___ ___ ___ ___ ___ ___ ___ ___ ___
 9   7   5   3   5   1   4   8   2   8   10   10   6   10

1.16 Bats

Even though most bats are helpful because they eat insects, few people like these winged creatures. What is an old, somewhat descriptive name for bats?

To answer the question, decide whether each sentence below is correct or a run-on sentence. Write the letter of each answer in the space above its sentence number at the bottom of the page.

1. Bats are winged mammals they are active at night.
   L. Correct sentence   R. Run-on

2. Most bats of North America hunt and eat insects.
   U. Correct sentence   I. Run-on

3. Bats fly swiftly and silently in search of food.
   I. Correct sentence   O. Run-on

4. A single bat may catch and eat a hundred insects or more in one night.
   M. Correct sentence   J. Run-on

5. Bats sleep during the day, they prefer caves, church towers, barns, and similar places.
   T. Correct sentence   L. Run-on

6. Some bats live in large colonies others live alone or in small groups.
   E. Correct sentence   S. Run-on

7. Bats rely on echolocation to fly through the darkness.
   F. Correct sentence   B. Run-on

8. Some people are frightened of bats, they believe bats attack people.
   L. Correct sentence   O. Run-on

9. Unless they are sick, bats are usually not dangerous.
   T. Correct sentence   P. Run-on

10. A bat appears suddenly in the night in an instant it is gone.
    U. Correct sentence   E. Run-on

___ ___ ___ ___ ___ ___ ___ ___ ___ ___ ___ ___
7   5   3   9   9   10   1   4   8   2   6   10

1.17 Reaching a Low Point

The lowest place in the United States is in California. What is the name of this place?

   To answer the question, decide whether each example below is a correct sentence, a run-on sentence, or a sentence fragment. Write the letter of each answer in the space above its number at the bottom of the page. You will need to divide the letters into words.

1. About 70 percent of the Earth's surface is covered with water the rest is land.
    R. Sentence   T. Run-on   C. Fragment

2. Of all the oceans, the Pacific is the largest.
    V. Sentence   U. Run-on   Y. Fragment

3. Mountains are found on every continent the highest mountain is in Asia.
    S. Sentence   A. Run-on   N. Fragment

4. Mount Everest in the Himalayas at nearly thirty thousand feet.
    D. Sentence   U. Run-on   H. Fragment

5. The Rocky Mountains run north to south, they divide the United States.
    D. Sentence   E. Run-on   R. Fragment

6. The surface of the Earth in slow but constant change.
    J. Sentence   R. Run-on   L. Fragment

7. Over time wind, rain, and changing temperatures.
    N. Sentence   S. Run-on   Y. Fragment

8. The surface features of our planet are truly remarkable.
    D. Sentence   S. Run-on   M. Fragment

___ ___ ___ ___ ___ ___ ___ ___ ___ ___ ___
 8   5   3   1   4   2   3   6   6   5   7

1.18 Guiding Light

Polaris, the last star in the handle of the constellation known as the Little Dipper, has been a guiding light for travelers for centuries. What is the common name of Polaris?

To answer the question, identify each sentence below with its most accurate label. Also identify run-on sentences and sentence fragments. Select your answers from the choices that follow the sentences. Write the letter of each answer in the space above the sentence number at the bottom of the page. You will need to divide the letters into words.

1. If you are outside on a clear night, a few thousand stars will be visible.

2. Do you know what a galaxy is?

3. A galaxy contains billions of stars, all of the stars of a galaxy travel through space together.

4. Billions of galaxies in the universe.

5. Our galaxy is called the Milky Way.

6. How wondrous the night sky is!

7. Our sun is a star, and it provides the Earth with light and heat.

8. Look for the stars on a clear night.

Answers

A.	Simple, declarative	H.	Compound
E.	Simple, interrogative	O.	Complex
T.	Simple, imperative	N.	Fragment
R.	Simple, exclamatory	S.	Run-on

___ ___ ___ ___ ___ ___ ___ ___ ___ ___ ___ ___
 8   7   2   4   1   6   8   7   3   8   5   6

1.19 Great Game

This board game, invented in 1933, is one of the bestselling games of all time. You and some of your friends have probably played it. What is the name of this game?

To answer the question, determine which parts of the sentences below are underlined. The underlined words might be a complete subject, complete predicate, simple subject, simple predicate, compound subject, or compound predicate. Match the underlined parts of the sentences with the terms that follow the sentences. Then write the letter of the term in the space above the sentence number at the bottom of the page.

1. Millions of people <u>play</u> games every day.

2. <u>Chess</u> and <u>checkers</u> were popular over a thousand years ago.

3. <u>Many games</u> require strategy and skill.

4. Other popular <u>games</u> are based on chance.

5. In recent years video games <u>have become very popular</u>.

6. <u>The popularity of video games</u> is likely to grow in the coming years.

7. Most video games <u>are</u> fun and <u>provide</u> great entertainment for players.

8. <u>Christina, who is Will's younger sister,</u> is an outstanding video game player.

Answers

O. Complete subject
Y. Complete predicate
P. Simple subject
N. Simple predicate
L. Compound subject
M. Compound predicate

$\overline{}$ $\overline{}$ $\overline{}$ $\overline{}$ $\overline{}$ $\overline{}$ $\overline{}$ $\overline{}$
7   3   1   8   4   6   2   5

Sentences

1.20 Magician

This man was one of the greatest magicians and escape artists of all time. He died on Halloween in 1926. Who was he?

To answer the question, determine whether each example below is a correctly written sentence. If the example is a correctly written sentence, write the letter for "correct" in the space above the example's number at the bottom of the page. If it is not a correctly written sentence, write the letter for "incorrect." You will need to divide the letters into words.

1. Tom is an amateur magician, he enjoys entertaining his friends.
   N. Correct   U. Incorrect

2. He has always liked fooling people with illusions.
   A. Correct   H. Incorrect

3. He practices each day.
   O. Correct   E. Incorrect

4. In hopes of perfecting his skill.
   I. Correct   N. Incorrect

5. Tom often performs at charity events.
   D. Correct   T. Incorrect

6. His favorite tricks involve cards.
   Y. Correct   A. Incorrect

7. Picking a card from a deck that matches a card a person picked earlier.
   N. Correct   I. Incorrect

8. Tom also likes making an egg disappear he then makes it reappear.
   L. Correct   R. Incorrect

9. For Tom, being a magician is a lot of fun.
   H. Correct   M. Incorrect

__	__	__	__	__	__	__	__	__	__	__	__
9	2	8	8	6	9	3	1	5	7	4	7

1.21 Presidential Photo

This president was the first to be photographed. Who was he?

To find the answer to the question, decide whether each statement below is true or false. If a statement is true, write the letter for "true" in the space above its number at the bottom of the page. If a statement is false, write the letter for "false." You will need to reverse and divide the letters into words.

1. To express a complete thought, a sentence must have a subject and predicate.
   E. True   N. False

2. There are five kinds of sentences in English.
   E. True   O. False

3. A sentence fragment is considered complete as long as it has a subject or a predicate.
   H. True   M. False

4. A compound subject must have a compound predicate.
   E. True   L. False

5. A declarative sentence is a statement.
   P. True   N. False

6. A simple subject may also be the complete subject.
   S. True   A. False

7. An exclamatory sentence may be followed by a period, question mark, or an exclamation point.
   S. True   K. False

8. An interrogative sentence asks a question.
   A. True   O. False

9. An independent clause cannot stand alone as a simple sentence.
   A. True   J. False

___ ___ ___ ___ ___ ___ ___ ___ ___
 7   4   2   5   6   1   3   8   9

Nouns

Nouns are words that name a person, place, thing, or idea. There are many different kinds of nouns your students should know.

The tip sheets and worksheets that follow will help your students in their study of nouns. The first tip sheet starts this section with a list and description of the eight parts of speech. You may want to distribute copies of this tip sheet to your students as a general review. The second tip sheet and Worksheets 2.1 through 2.5 focus on singular and plural nouns, and common and proper nouns. The third tip sheet and Worksheets 2.6 and 2.7 focus on irregular plural nouns. The final tip sheet and Worksheets 2.8 through 2.10 cover possessive nouns, and Worksheets 2.11 through 2.14 offer a review of nouns.

The Parts of Speech

Each word in English can be classified according to the way it is used in a sentence. Some words may be used only one way. Others may be used in more than one way. When we refer to the *parts of speech*, we are speaking of the different ways words are used in sentences. There are eight parts of speech.

- Noun: names a person, place, thing, or idea

  Examples: James, sister, sky, rabbit, freedom

- Verb: shows action or state of being

  Examples: walk, run, is, were

- Pronoun: takes the place of a noun

  Examples: I, you, he, she, it, they, them, anybody

- Adjective: describes a noun or pronoun

  Examples: little, happy, silly, big

- Adverb: describes a verb, adjective, or another adverb

  Examples: suddenly, now, quietly, quickly, very

- Conjunction: joins words or groups of words

  Examples: and, but, or, yet, as, although, when

- Preposition: relates a noun or pronoun to other words in a sentence

  Examples: from, in, on, to, below

- Interjection: shows strong feeling or emotion

  Examples: Oh no! Wow! Look out!

Nouns

A *noun* names a person, place, thing, or idea. There are many different kinds of nouns:

- *Common nouns* name any person, place, thing, or idea.

  Examples: boy, girl, school, city, ocean, mountain, democracy

- *Proper nouns* name a particular person, place, thing, or idea.

  Examples: John, Mary, the United States of America, North America, Mississippi River, Golden Gate Bridge, Mexico, Pacific Ocean

- *Singular nouns* name one person, place, thing, or idea.

  Examples: student, day, night, kitten, town, church, valley, city, potato

- *Plural nouns* name more than one person, place, thing, or idea. Most plural nouns form their plural by adding *-s* or *-es*.

  Examples: students, days, nights, kittens, towns, churches, valleys, cities, potatoes

- *Possessive nouns* show ownership by adding an apostrophe and *-s* or just an apostrophe. They can be singular or plural.

  Examples: Charles's book, the cat's pillow, the girls' soccer team, the puppies' dish, the children's toys

- *Count nouns* name things that can be counted. These nouns have plural forms.

  Examples: trees, rivers, students, towns, books

- *Noncount nouns*, also known as *mass nouns*, name things that are not usually counted. (Although noncount nouns have plural forms—for example, the sands of the world's deserts—these forms are seldom used.)

  Examples: snow, anger, love, health, sand

- *Collective nouns* name a group of persons, places, or things.

  Examples: crowd, herd, team, audience

2.1 Short Presidency

This president had the shortest term of any president of the United States. He died after only one month in office. Who was he?

To answer the question, find the noun in each set of words below. Write the letter of the noun in the space above its line number at the bottom of the page. You will need to divide the letters into words.

1. U. wonderful   D. from   M. river   Z. little
2. O. essays   H. attempted   L. ran   I. careful
3. K. into   Y. schemed   O. detect   E. candidates
4. T. questioned   P. smiled   R. dessert   B. often
5. E. quickly   A. galaxies   I. spoke   W. helpless
6. U. icy   S. mosquito   E. invented   V. eat
7. Y. avenues   U. shrieked   Y. revise   O. harsh
8. E. molten   A. deserted   I. democracy   R. suddenly
9. T. galloping   E. erupt   M. smallest   N. device
10. J. myself   H. amphibians   K. softly   R. flew
11. W. liberty   V. mountainous   B. ancient   S. they
12. P. terrible   T. hopeful   L. audience   N. coarse

___ ___ ___ ___ ___ ___ ___ ___ ___ ___ ___ ___ ___ ___ ___ ___ ___ ___ ___ ___
11 8 12 12 8 5 1 10 3 9 4 7 10 5 4 4 8 6 2 9

2.2 Big Animal

About 110 feet long and weighing approximately 210 tons, this mammal is the world's biggest animal. What is its name?

   To answer the question, find a noun in each of the sentences below. Choose your answers from among the underlined words. Write the letter beneath the noun in the space above its sentence number at the bottom of the page. You will need to divide the letters into words.

1. Megan <u>chose</u> a <u>topic</u> <u>for</u> <u>her</u> science report.
         E   A   O U

2. <u>She</u> has <u>always</u> been <u>interested</u> in <u>animals</u>.
     S   N   R   B

3. <u>She</u> <u>finds</u> <u>bears</u> to be <u>fascinating</u> creatures.
     G C E   S

4. Bears <u>were</u> <u>once</u> found <u>throughout</u> the <u>country</u>.
         S Y   D   E

5. Natalie, Megan's <u>friend</u>, is <u>doing</u> <u>her</u> report <u>on</u> sea life.
                L   H T   C

6. Natalie <u>finds</u> sea life to <u>be</u> an <u>interesting</u> <u>subject</u>.
        N   L   B   H

7. The <u>biggest</u> animals in the <u>world</u> <u>are</u> <u>found</u> in the sea.
        R   L   U C

8. The girls <u>found</u> <u>much</u> of <u>their</u> information on the <u>Internet</u>.
          M   R   T   U

9. <u>They</u> <u>discovered</u> many <u>fascinating</u> <u>facts</u> about animals.
     E   S   C   W

___ ___ ___ ___ ___ ___ ___ ___ ___
 2   5   8   3   9   6   1   7   4

Nouns

2.3 Early Computer

In the 1830s, this mathematician and inventor built a mechanical computing machine that many people consider to be an early computer. Who was he?

To answer the question, find the underlined common or proper noun in each sentence below. Only one noun is underlined in each sentence. Write the letter of the noun in the space above its sentence number at the bottom of the page. You will need to divide the letters into words.

1. Elisa has <u>always</u> <u>been</u> <u>interested</u> in <u>computers</u>.
              T   D   N   S

2. <u>She</u> <u>chose</u> computers as the <u>topic</u> for <u>her</u> science report.
   N   L   R   E

3. An <u>early</u> <u>computing</u> machine was <u>built</u> in <u>England</u> in the 1830s.
      E   T   W   H

4. The <u>inventor</u> <u>was</u> a <u>noted</u> <u>mathematician</u>.
      M   S   E   G

5. On <u>Saturday</u> Elisa <u>told</u> her friend Rachel <u>about</u> <u>this</u> invention.
      L   H   C   R

6. The girls <u>decided</u> to <u>find</u> <u>more</u> information on the <u>Internet</u>.
        T   S   K   C

7. <u>They</u> <u>finished</u> their research <u>late</u> in the <u>day</u>.
  N   D   S   E

8. Elisa's mom <u>invited</u> <u>Rachel</u> to <u>stay</u> and have dinner with <u>them</u>.
          I   A   J   O

9. Elisa's <u>mom</u> <u>prepared</u> an <u>excellent</u> <u>meal</u>.
      B   G   T   M

___ ___ ___ ___ ___ ___ ___ ___ ___ ___ ___ ___ ___ ___
 6   3   8   2   5   7   1   9   8   9   9   8   4   7

Nouns

2.4 More Than an Inventor

This man is famous for inventing one of the world's most important devices. But he also was one of the founders of the National Geographic Society. Who was he?

To answer the question, match the singular noun with its plural form. Write the letter of each answer in the space above its number at the bottom of the page. You will need to divide the letters into words.

1. dish
   S. dishs   N. dishes   C. dishies

2. family
   R. families   M. familys   L. familes

3. mountain
   P. mountaines   M. mountains   T. mountainies

4. valley
   H. valleyes   S. vallies   D. valleys

5. hero
   V. heros   H. heroes   I. heroies

6. thief
   B. thieves   E. thiefs   M. thievs

7. country
   U. countrys   A. countryes   E. countries

8. calf
   T. calvies   J. calfs   G. calves

9. potato
   A. potatoes   I. potatos   R. potato

10. roof
    V. roofes   X. roofs   Z. rooves

11. journey
    J. journeyes   Y. journies   L. journeys

___ ___ ___ ___ ___ ___ ___ ___ ___ ___ ___ ___ ___ ___ ___ ___ ___ ___
9   11 7   10 9   1   4   7   2   8   2   9   5   9   3   6   7   11 11

Nouns

2.5 Early Flyers

According to Greek mythology, a father and son were imprisoned on the island of Crete. They attempted to escape by building wings and flying away. What were their names?

To answer the question, complete each sentence below with the correct form of the plural noun. Choose your answers from the words following each sentence. Write the letter of each plural noun in the space above its sentence number at the bottom of the page. You will need to divide the letters into words.

1. Greek mythology contains many fascinating _____.
   L. stories   U. storys

2. Many myths were about the _____ of heroes and heroines.
   N. lifes   S. lives

3. Some myths arose from the religious _____ of the people.
   T. believes   N. beliefs

4. Gods and _____ were characters in many myths.
   C. goddesss   R. goddesses

5. The characters in myths often had to perform great _____ of courage.
   E. feats   I. feates

6. Many myths tried to explain the _____ of nature.
   I. wonders   A. wonderes

7. Most myths ended as _____ for the characters.
   E. tragedys   U. tragedies

8. A few myths had happy _____.
   D. endings   M. endinges

9. _____ believe that some myths may have been loosely based on real events.
   C. Historians   J. Historianes

10. Myths tell us much about _____ of the ancient world.
    E. societys   A. societies

___ ___ ___ ___ ___ ___ ___ ___ ___ ___ ___ ___ ___ ___ ___ ___
 8 10 5   8 10   1   7   2 10   3   8   6   9 10   4   7   2

Irregular Nouns

The plural forms of most nouns are made by adding -s or -es. The plurals of irregular nouns are not made in this way. Most irregular nouns change their form from the singular to the plural; some stay the same.

The following are examples of the singular and plural forms of common irregular nouns:

child–children	axis–axes
foot–feet	louse–lice
mouse–mice	die–dice
goose–geese	crisis–crises
ox–oxen	oasis–oases
man–men	tooth–teeth
woman–women	radius–radii
medium–media	basis–bases
parenthesis–parentheses	larva–larvae

The following are examples of nouns that have the same singular and plural forms:

sheep–sheep	cod–cod
moose–moose	species–species
deer–deer	bass–bass
trout–trout	barley–barley
series–series	salmon–salmon
traffic–traffic	wheat–wheat

2.6 Paying for Parking

The first parking meter was installed in 1935. Where was it installed?

To answer the question, match each singular noun with its plural form. Write the letter of each answer in the space above its number at the bottom of the page. You will need to divide the letters into words.

1. woman
   R. womans   A. women   U. womanes

2. mouse
   I. mouses   H. mousies   O. mice

3. sheep
   A. sheep   E. sheeps   M. sheepes

4. ox
   L. oxens   C. oxes   H. oxen

5. child
   O. childs   I. children   U. childrens

6. piano
   I. pianoes   L. pianos   N. piano

7. foot
   M. feet   R. feets   D. foots

8. goose
   T. geese   E. gander   I. geeses

9. traffic
   H. traffics   R. traffices   K. traffic

10. tooth
    N. toothes   S. tooths   C. teeth

11. deer
    O. deer   S. deers   B. doe

12. radius
    N. radiuss   Y. radii   D. radius

___ ___ ___ ___ ___ ___ ___ ___ ___ ___ ___ ___
 11   9   6   3   4   2   7   1   10   5   8   12

Nouns

2.7 Unofficial National Anthem

"America the Beautiful" is often called the unofficial national anthem of the United States. Who wrote the original poem in 1895 that was eventually set to music and became this famous song?

To answer the question, match each singular noun with its plural form. Write the letter of each answer in the space above its number at the bottom of the page. You will need to divide the letters into words.

1. moose
   E. meese   I. moose   U. mooses

2. crisis
   S. crises   D. crisi   N. crisises

3. oasis
   L. oases   K. oasis   R. oasises

4. man
   Y. mans   E. mens   H. men

5. series
   I. seri   A. series   E. seriess

6. salmon
   Z. salmen   M. salmones   R. salmon

7. auto
   B. autos   Y. autoes   P. auti

8. die
   C. dies   N. dice   J. dices

9. wheat
   H. wheats   T. wheat   U. wheaties

10. species
    I. speci   A. specis   E. species

11. solo
    K. solos   S. soloes   M. solois

___ ___ ___ ___ ___ ___ ___ ___ ___ ___ ___ ___ ___ ___ ___ ___
11   5   9   4   10 6   1   8   10 3   10 10 7   5   9   10 2

Nouns

Possessive Nouns

. . . .

Possessive nouns show ownership. They indicate that a thing belongs to someone or something. Apostrophes are used to show the possessive case. Possessive nouns may be singular or plural.

- To write the possessive form of singular nouns, add an apostrophe and -s.

    Examples: Sue's coat, Charles's book, the bird's cage, Oregon's forests

    Exception: When a word of more than one syllable ends in an "s" sound, the singular possessive may be formed by adding only an apostrophe. This eliminates awkward pronunciations.

    Examples: Moses' leadership, Ms. Rogers' office, the witness' account of the accident

- To write the possessive form of plural nouns that end in -s, add only an apostrophe.

    Examples: the two sisters' bikes, the puppies' bed, the boys' locker room, the Johnsons' house

- To write the possessive form of plural nouns that do not end in -s, add an apostrophe and -s.

    Examples: the men's ski team, the children's toys, the mice's nest

. . . .

2.8 Superparents

Superman (Clark Kent) was born on Krypton. His adoptive Earth parents were Martha and Jonathan Kent. What were the names of his real parents?

To answer the question, match each singular noun with its singular possessive or plural possessive form. Write the letter of each answer in the space above the number of the singular noun at the bottom of the page. You will need to divide the letters into words.

1. reporter (singular possessive)
   K. reporters'   S. reporters's   A. reporter's

2. spaceship (singular possessive)
   R. spaceship's   I. spaceships'   Y. spaceships's

3. Clark (singular possessive)
   U. Clarks'   E. Clarkes'   R. Clark's

4. planet (plural possessive)
   U. planet's   D. planets'   O. planetes'

5. farm (singular possessive)
   L. farms'   D. farms's   A. farm's

6. truth (plural possessive)
   I. truth's   O. truths'   U. truthes'

7. friend (plural possessive)
   E. friendes'   H. friend's   A. friends'

8. villain (singular possessive)
   Y. villains'   L. villain's   R. villaines'

9. child (plural possessive)
   S. childrens'   N. children's   P. child's

10. city (plural possessive)
    G. cities's   D. city's   L. cities'

11. Lois (singular possessive)
    J. Lois'   Y. Loises'   N. Loisies'

12. hero (plural possessive)
    I. hero's   E. heroes'   R. heros'

___ ___ ___ ___ ___ ___ ___ ___ ___ ___ - ___ ___
10   7   2   5   1   9   4   11 6   3   12 8

Nouns

2.9 Great Organization

In 1881, Clara Barton founded an organization that has since helped millions of people. What organization did she start?

To answer the question, find the two correct possessive forms of nouns in each line. These two nouns may both be singular or plural, or they may be a singular noun and a plural noun. Starting with the first letter of your answers, write the letters in order in the spaces at the bottom of the page. When you are done, reverse and divide the letters into words.

1. N. canyons's   S. students'   I. mens'   S. family's

2. O. people's   G. wifes'   T. coachs'   R. tourists'

3. C. museum's   D. children's   U. deers'   M. turkies'

4. E. passengers'   H. countrys'   N. babys'   R. diplomat's

5. W. wolve's   N. continent's   A. Lisa's   S. citys'

6. C. foxes'   D. womans'   I. bridge's   P. towns's

7. L. walruses's   C. thieve's   R. storm's   E. schools'

8. M. officers'   V. dentists's   A. champion's   U. classes's

— — — — — — — — — — — — — — — — —

2.10 Final Frontier

On May 5, 1961, this man became the first American to fly into space. Although the flight lasted only fifteen minutes, it began the manned space program for the United States. Who was this astronaut?

To answer the question, find the singular or plural possessive noun in each sentence below. Decide whether the possessive noun is used correctly. If it is correct, write the letter for "correct" in the space above its sentence number at the bottom of the page. If it is incorrect, write the letter for "incorrect." You will need to divide the letters into words.

1. Jason's group presented an oral report to the class about the space program.
   E. Correct   I. Incorrect

2. The dream of space flight has excited people's imaginations for thousands of years.
   R. Correct   N. Incorrect

3. Each of the groupes' members presented a part of the report.
   X. Correct   N. Incorrect

4. A rocket's powerful engines are needed to lift spacecraft into orbit.
   S. Correct   T. Incorrect

5. The astronauts's training is long and difficult.
   S. Correct   D. Incorrect

6. Danielle's portion of the report focused on the Apollo moon landings.
   L. Correct   O. Incorrect

7. The Apollo missions have unlocked some of the moons' secrets.
   M. Correct   P. Incorrect

8. The other students' questions were thoughtful.
   H. Correct   R. Incorrect

9. The classes's presentation about the space program was enjoyable and informative.
   J. Correct   A. Incorrect

___ ___ ___ ___ ___ ___ ___ ___ ___ ___ ___
 9   6   9   3   4   8   1   7   9   2   5

Nouns

© Gary Robert Muschla

Name _____   Date _____

2.11 Seventh Planet

Uranus was the first planet to be discovered with a telescope. Who discovered it?

   To answer the question, read the article below and determine whether the underlined words are nouns. (Not all nouns in the article are underlined.) Starting with the first sentence, write the letters beneath the nouns in order on the blanks at the bottom of the page. You will need to divide the letters into words.

Uranus, the <u>seventh</u> <u>planet</u>, was <u>discovered</u> in 1781 beyond the orbit of <u>Saturn</u>.
　　　　　　　T　　　　W　　　　　　　H　　　　　　　　　　　　　　　　　I

Uranus is <u>about</u> four times as big as <u>Earth</u> and lies about 1.78 billion <u>miles</u> from the sun.
　　　　　　　O　　　　　　　　　　　　　L　　　　　　　　　　　　　　　　L

It <u>takes</u> Uranus about eighty-four <u>years</u> to make a <u>complete</u> trip around the sun.
　　M　　　　　　　　　　　　　　　I　　　　　　　　　A

<u>Although</u> <u>astronomers</u> do not know <u>much</u> about the <u>surface</u> of the <u>planet</u>, they
　　S　　　　　A　　　　　　　　　D　　　　　　　M　　　　　　H

<u>know</u> that its <u>atmosphere</u> is made up <u>mostly</u> of hydrogen, <u>helium</u>, and methane.
　T　　　　　　E　　　　　　　　　H　　　　　　　　R

Through a <u>telescope</u> Uranus <u>appears</u> to be a <u>bluish-green</u> <u>disk</u>, but <u>its</u> <u>color</u> is not
　　　　　　S　　　　　　U　　　　　　　　G　　　　C　　　M　H

<u>due</u> to any plant life or <u>oceans</u>. The average <u>temperature</u> on the planet is −350
　I　　　　　　　　　　　　E　　　　　　　　　L

degrees Fahrenheit (−214 degrees Celsius). Uranus is a cold, <u>inhospitable</u> world.
　　　　　　　　　　　　　　　　　　　　　　　　　　　　　　D

— — — — — — — — — — — — — — — — — —

42

© Gary Robert Muschla

2.12 Food for a Hearty Breakfast

Cereal is a popular breakfast food. Most cereal in the United States is produced in a Michigan city. What is the name of this city?

To answer the question, match the noun on the left with the most accurate label of its type on the right. Write the letter of each answer in the space above the noun's number at the bottom of the page. You will need to divide the letters into words.

Noun	Type
1. hawks	T. singular, common
2. Americans	E. plural, common
3. John's	K. singular, proper
4. Marianna	R. plural, proper
5. cougar	C. plural, irregular
6. spectators	L. singular possessive
7. children's	A. plural possessive
8. tomatoes	B. collective, common
9. flock	
10. geese	
11. village	

___ ___ ___ ___ ___ ___ ___ ___ ___ ___ ___
 9   7   5   11   3   1   10   2   8   6   4

Nouns

2.13 Walking on Four Feet

Animals such as dogs, horses, and elephants that walk on four feet belong to a special group. What is the name for animals that walk on four feet?

   To answer the question, complete each sentence below with the correct form of the noun. Choose your answers from the words that follow each sentence. Write the letter of each answer in the space above its sentence number at the bottom of the page.

1. _____ organisms can be divided into five major groups.
   M. Earths   E. Earth's

2. Each major group, called a _____, contains millions of different organisms.
   O. Kingdom   A. kingdom

3. All _____ belong to the Kingdom Animalia.
   P. animals   Y. animal

4. This large group is broken down into several _____.
   M. subgroupes   S. subgroups

5. A _____ is the smallest group of animals.
   R. species   S. speci

6. Some animals in _____ are in danger of becoming extinct.
   H. north America   U. North America

7. When _____ habitats are destroyed, the animals may have trouble surviving.
   Q. animals'   P. animal's

8. Environmentalists try to raise _____ awareness of habitat destruction.
   N. peoplies'   D. people's

__ __ __ __ __ __ __ __ __ __
 7   6   2   8   5   6   3   1   8   4

Nouns

2.14 Baseball Poem

In 1888, Ernest L. Thayer wrote a poem about baseball. What was the title of this poem?

To find the answer to the question, decide whether each statement below is true or false. If a statement is true, write the letter for "true" in the space above its number at the bottom of the page. If a statement is false, write the letter for "false." You will need to divide the letters into words.

1. A singular noun names only one person, place, thing, or idea, but a plural noun names one, two, or more.
   O. True   H. False

2. Nouns may be common or proper.
   E. True   O. False

3. Possessive nouns show ownership.
   S. True   E. False

4. Only plural possessive nouns that do not end in -s require an apostrophe.
   A. True   B. False

5. An example of an irregular plural noun is "puppies."
   L. True   Y. False

6. A collective noun names a group, for example "audience."
   A. True   H. False

7. A proper noun does not always have to be capitalized.
   T. True   C. False

8. The singular and plural forms for some irregular nouns are the same.
   T. True   E. False

___ ___ ___ ___ ___ ___ ___ ___ ___ ___ ___ ___ ___
 7   6   3   2   5   6   8   8   1   2   4   6   8

Nouns

Verbs

Verbs are words that express action or state of being. Along with a subject, every sentence must have a verb.

The following tip sheets and worksheets address the essential concepts for understanding verbs and verb usage. The first tip sheet and Worksheets 3.1 through 3.10 cover action verbs, linking verbs, and verb phrases. The second tip sheet and Worksheets 3.11 through 3.15 focus on direct and indirect objects. The third tip sheet and Worksheets 3.16 through 3.18 concentrate on predicate nominatives and predicate adjectives, while Worksheet 3.19 concentrates on verb contractions. The fourth tip sheet and Worksheets 3.20 and 3.21 cover verb tenses, the fifth tip sheet and Worksheets 3.22 through 3.25 address irregular verbs, and the sixth tip sheet and Worksheets 3.26 through 3.29 cover subject and verb agreement. Finally, Worksheets 3.30 through 3.32 provide reviews of verbs.

Two Kinds of Verbs

Verbs are words that express action or state of being.

- *Action verbs* tell what the subject of a sentences does:

  Tony *writes* a sports column for the school newspaper.

  Susan *read* two novels last week.

  The hawk *flew* over the field in search of prey.

- *State-of-being verbs,* also known as *linking verbs,* show the condition or state of a person or thing. They link the subject with a word in the predicate. Forms of the verb *be—am, is, are, was, were, being,* and *been—*are linking verbs:

  Tyrel *was* happy.

  Juan *is* an excellent baseball player.

  I *am* hungry.

- Other verbs such as *appear, become, feel, grow, sound, seem, look,* and *taste* can also serve as linking verbs. To serve as linking verbs, these verbs must be used in a sentence in which they can take the place of the verb *be*:

  Larissa *seemed* surprised.

  Larissa *was* surprised.

  The puppies *look* sleepy.

  The puppies *are* sleepy.

- A verb that contains more than one word is called a *verb phrase.* The last word in the phrase is the *main verb.* All other words in the phrase are *helping verbs.* There are several helping verbs: *am, are, is, was, were, be, being, been, have, has, had, do, does, did, will, would, shall, should, can, could, may, might,* and *must.*

  Tom *had made* several careless mistakes on his test.

  Maria *may finish* her report by Friday.

  We *will be going* to the movies tonight.

3.1 Legendary Schoolteacher

One of Washington Irving's most famous stories is "The Legend of Sleepy Hollow." In this story, a schoolteacher becomes convinced that a headless horseman is chasing him. What was the name of this schoolteacher?

To answer the question, find the action verb in each set of words below. Write the letter of the action verb in the space above its line number at the bottom of the page.

1. O. theater   U. tornado   H. find   Y. suddenly

2. E. several   N. called   I. brightest   C. starlight

3. K. directions   S. computer   D. horrible   R. traveled

4. O. eat   E. sunrise   U. early   I. somebody

5. M. printer   T. delightful   B. caught   H. partner

6. A. beautiful   R. farther   C. designed   E. temperature

7. D. through   E. climbed   S. luckily   Y. happiness

8. I. current   U. lieutenant   H. nervous   A. rode

9. I. borrow   M. heavy   C. plentiful   T. warmer

10. E. along   N. information   M. numerous   D. sang

___ ___ ___ ___ ___ ___ ___   ___ ___ ___ ___ ___
 9   6   1   8   5   4   10   6   3   8   2   7

Verbs

3.2 Special Group of Animals

Animals such as kangaroos that carry their young in a pouch have a special name. What is it?

To answer the question, find the action verb in each sentence below. Choose your answers from among the underlined words. Write the letter beneath the verb in the space above its sentence number at the bottom of the page.

1. Many <u>strange</u> <u>creatures</u> <u>live</u> on the <u>continent</u> of Australia.
        U   T   I   M

2. Numerous <u>species</u> of kangaroos <u>thrive</u> in Australia <u>and</u> on <u>nearby</u> islands.
        I   A   R   H

3. Kangaroos <u>range</u> in <u>size</u> <u>from</u> <u>small</u> wallabies to great gray kangaroos.
      U   A   Y   N

4. Great <u>gray</u> kangaroos <u>reach</u> a <u>height</u> of <u>about</u> five feet.
      K   P   T   V

5. A <u>large</u> kangaroo <u>jumps</u> <u>up</u> to twenty-five <u>feet</u> in a single leap.
   N   S D   R

6. <u>Female</u> kangaroos <u>carry</u> their <u>young</u> in their <u>pouches</u>.
   G   L   E   R

7. After <u>several</u> weeks, a <u>young</u> kangaroo <u>leaves</u> its <u>mother's</u> pouch.
    H   E   R   T

8. The <u>first</u> <u>European</u> <u>explorers</u> <u>observed</u> kangaroos in 1682.
   R   N   U   A

9. They <u>returned</u> to Europe <u>with</u> <u>stories</u> of <u>these</u> strange animals.
   M   R   L   T

10. Many <u>people</u> <u>think</u> that kangaroos <u>are</u> <u>interesting</u> animals.
    K   S   N   T

___ ___ ___ ___ ___ ___ ___ ___ ___ ___
9   2   7   10   3   4   1   8   6   5

Verbs

3.3 Getting Goosebumps

R. L. Stine is the author of the famous Goosebumps series. What do the initials R. L. stand for?

  To answer the question, find the action verb in each sentence below. In the parentheses that follow each sentence, a letter is called for. Find this letter in the verb, then write the letter in the space above the verb's sentence number at the bottom of the page. The first one is done for you. You will need to divide the letters into words.

1. Many people **r**ead scary horror stories. (first letter)

2. Melissa's favorite stories contain ghosts and hideous creatures. (fifth letter)

3. She thinks some of the Goosebumps stories are delightfully terrifying. (first letter)

4. Her friend Leah worries about nightmares because of these stories. (first letter)

5. Melissa considers these kinds of stories fun. (second letter)

6. Great stories always capture her imagination. (first letter)

7. The girls like horror movies too. (first letter)

8. Last week Melissa borrowed a novel about ghosts from Leah. (first letter)

9. She finished the entire book in one day. (third letter)

10. The next day she returned the book to Leah. (second letter)

11. Leah offered Melissa another book. (fifth letter)

R	__	__	__	__	__	__	__	__	__	__	__	__	__
1	5	8	10	11	3	7	2	4	11	10	9	6	10

Verbs

3.4 Start of a Great Career

In 1928, Mickey Mouse's career began when he starred in the first animated cartoon that had sound. What was the title of this cartoon?

To answer the question, find the verb phrase in each sentence below. In the parentheses that follow each sentence, a letter is called for. Find this letter in the verb phrase, then write the letter in the space above the phrase's sentence number at the bottom of the page. The first one is done for you. You will need to divide the letters into words.

1. The cartoon character of Mickey Mouse <u>was intro</u>duced by Walt Disney in 1928. (eighth letter)

2. Walt Disney was born in Chicago on December 5, 1901. (fourth letter)

3. As early as 1923, he was developing animated motion pictures. (third letter)

4. These early animated cartoons were produced without sound. (first letter)

5. Mickey Mouse was featured in the first animated cartoon that had sound. (fifth letter)

6. Mickey has become one of the world's most famous cartoon characters. (eighth letter)

7. Walt Disney has created several other famous cartoon characters. (eighth letter)

8. These characters have starred in numerous movies and cartoons. (seventh letter)

9. Certainly they will be in many more. (second letter)

10. Many of Walt Disney's characters are loved by children around the world. (fourth letter)

__	__	__	__	__	__	O	__	__	__	__	__	__	__
3	7	5	8	6	2	1	8	7	4	9	10	10	9	5

Verbs

3.5 Unusual Mammal

This unusual mammal does not bear live young. Its young hatch from eggs. What is the name of this mammal?

To answer the question, read the article below and determine whether the underlined phrases are verb phrases. Starting with the first sentence, write the letters beneath the verb phrases in order on the blanks at the bottom of the page.

There <u>are about</u> forty-two hundred species of mammals. Mammals <u>have become</u> the
      M   P

dominant life forms on Earth. Dogs, cats, horses, dolphins, bats, and humans

<u>are examples</u> of mammals. Unlike other animals, mammals <u>can adapt</u> to different
     O   L

environments. They <u>are found</u> throughout the world in many habitats. From the poles
                 A

to the equator, mammals <u>have populated</u> the world. Mammals <u>share distinct</u>
                              T   N

characteristics. The bodies of mammals <u>are covered</u> with hair. Mammals <u>nourish their</u>
                                    Y   S

young with milk. Most mammals <u>give birth to live</u> young. One of their most important
                                  T

characteristics <u>is being</u> warm-blooded. Their bodies <u>are kept</u> at a constant temperature.
                          P   U

This <u>helps mammals</u> to live in both cold and warm climates. Because of their unique
               E

characteristics, mammals <u>will remain</u> the dominant life forms on our planet.
                         S

___   ___   ___   ___   ___   ___   ___   ___   ___

Verbs

3.6 Extinct Bird

This extinct bird was once thought to be the most numerous bird in North America. What was the name of this bird?

To answer the question, read each sentence below and determine whether the underlined verb is a linking verb. If the verb is a linking verb, write the letter for "yes" in the space above its sentence number at the bottom of the page. If the verb is not a linking verb, write the letter for "no." You will need to divide the letters into words.

1. Birds <u>are</u> the only animals with feathers.
   I. Yes   H. No

2. Not all birds <u>possess</u> the ability to fly.
   U. Yes   A. No

3. Dinosaurs <u>were</u> the ancestors of birds.
   R. Yes   S. No

4. Birds <u>share</u> some characteristics with mammals.
   E. Yes   O. No

5. Being warm-blooded <u>is</u> one of these characteristics.
   N. Yes   L. No

6. Baby birds <u>begin</u> their lives by hatching from eggs.
   T. Yes   G. No

7. Birds <u>live</u> on every continent and most islands of the world.
   M. Yes   E. No

8. Scientists <u>know</u> of about nine thousand species of birds.
   H. Yes   P. No

9. Sara's grandfather <u>was</u> an ornithologist, a scientist who studies birds.
   S. Yes   M. No

__ __ __ __ __ __ __ __ __ __ __ __ __ __ __ __
 8 2 9 9 7 5 6 7 3 8 1 6 7 4 5

Verbs

3.7 Not Quite Baseball

In 1953, David Mullany invented a famous toy. What was it?

  To answer the question, find the linking verb in each sentence below. Choose your answers from among the underlined words. Write the letter beneath each linking verb in the space above its sentence number at the bottom of the page. You will need to divide the letters into words.

1. Clarise is an excellent softball player.
   E H   F   R

2. Last year she was an all-star for her middle school team.
   N   D   L   U

3. This year Clarise became the star of her high school team.
   U   I   A O

4. During a game Clarise always seems confident.
   Y   R   A   E

5. Deep inside, though, she feels nervous before a game.
   O   L   F   S

6. Many of her friends and fans were at her last game.
   B   H   L P

7. I am one of Clarise's fans.
   L B S   N

8. Her friends, of course, are some of her biggest fans.
   I   R   B   C

9. Clarise is also a polite, considerate person.
   F T   E   M

10. Even with all her success, she remains a great friend.
    H P   I   W

___ ___ ___ ___ ___ ___ ___ ___ ___ ___
10   3   5   9   6   1   8   4   2   7

Verbs

3.8 Famous Engineer

Most people have heard of Casey Jones, the famous railroad engineer who has become a part of American folklore. Most do not know that the story of Casey Jones was based on a real railroad engineer who was born near Cayce, Kentucky. What was this man's full name?

    To answer the question, find the action or linking verb in each set of words below. Write the letter of the verb in the space above its line number at the bottom of the page. You will need to divide the letters into words.

1. Action: E. abundant   U. predict   A. condition   O. been

2. Linking: S. colonel   V. construct   L. elusive   R. were

3. Action: M. was   R. information   B. humble   T. climb

4. Action: N. revise   R. gallantly   J. destiny   S. agent

5. Linking: H. factor   L. is   R. heroic   T. produce

6. Action: I. were   A. stubborn   E. invent   U. mountain

7. Linking: H. are   N. tragedy   S. develop   R. fearless

8. Action: T. courage   J. express   R. be   S. collision

9. Linking: H. remember   U. story   O. am   I. magnificent

___ ___ ___ ___ ___ ___ ___ ___ ___ ___ Jones
 8   9   7   4   5   1   3   7   6   2

Verbs

3.9 Speaking Of . . .

With more than one billion speakers, this language has more speakers than any other. What is the name of this language?

To answer the question, decide whether the underlined verb in each sentence is an action verb or a linking verb. If a verb is an action verb, write the letter for "action" in the space above its sentence number at the bottom of the page. If a verb is a linking verb, write the letter for "linking."

1. Over twenty-five hundred languages <u>are</u> common around the world.
   S. Action   R. Linking

2. Many people <u>know</u> two or more languages.
   N. Action   G. Linking

3. Maria <u>converses</u> in English and Spanish fluently.
   I. Action   H. Linking

4. As a young child, she <u>learned</u> both languages at home from her parents.
   A. Action   N. Linking

5. Of all the children in her family only Maria <u>is</u> bilingual.
   I. Action   A. Linking

6. Maria's grandfather and grandmother <u>were</u> bilingual too.
   S. Action   N. Linking

7. Last year Maria <u>studied</u> both English and Spanish in school.
   M. Action   E. Linking

8. She <u>feels</u> comfortable speaking either language.
   L. Action   D. Linking

| ___ | ___ | ___ | ___ | ___ | ___ | ___ | ___ |
| 7 | 4 | 2 | 8 | 5 | 1 | 3 | 6 |

Verbs

3.10 Name Change

Helena, the capital of Montana, was originally a mining town in the 1860s. Back then, the town was not called Helena. What was Helena's original name?

To answer the question, find the verb in each sentence below. Decide whether the verb is an action verb or a linking verb. If a verb is an action verb, write the letter for "action" in the space above its sentence number at the bottom of the page. If a verb is a linking verb, write the letter for "linking." You will need to divide the letters into words.

1. Many frontier towns in the Old West were mining towns.
   R. Action   N. Linking

2. Living on the frontier was difficult and dangerous.
   U. Action   S. Linking

3. Early miners dreamed of becoming rich one day.
   L. Action   M. Linking

4. Most found only hardship and disappointment.
   E. Action   T. Linking

5. Many miners grew disillusioned with their dreams of wealth.
   S. Action   U. Linking

6. In time many of the mining towns became deserted.
   N. Action   T. Linking

7. Some towns developed as centers of trade on the frontier.
   H. Action   S. Linking

8. People moved to these towns in hopes of starting new lives.
   G. Action   R. Linking

9. Today some of the early mining towns are major cities.
   T. Action   C. Linking

10. Most of the current residents know little of the history of these places.
    A. Action   O. Linking

___ ___ ___ ___ ___ ___ ___ ___ ___ ___ ___ ___ ___ ___ ___
3   10   2   6   9   7   10   1   9   4   8   5   3   9   7

Verbs

Direct and Indirect Objects

In many sentences, words after the verb complete the action named by the verb. These words may be *direct objects* or *indirect objects*. Here are some facts about and examples of direct objects:

- A direct object usually is a noun or pronoun.

- A direct object follows an action verb and receives the action of the verb. Verbs that have direct objects are called *transitive verbs*. Verbs that do not have direct objects are called *intransitive verbs*.

- A direct object answers the question *whom*? or *what*?

- A sentence may have one, two, or more direct objects:

  Jessica called me from her cell phone. (Whom did Jessica call? *Me.*)

  Sue plays the guitar and piano. (What does Sue play? *Guitar* and *piano.*)

Some verbs also have an indirect object. Here are some facts about and examples of indirect objects:

- An indirect object usually is a noun or pronoun.

- An indirect object always comes before a direct object. Only verbs that have a direct object can have an indirect object (but a verb that has a direct object may not have an indirect object).

- An indirect object answers the questions *to whom?, for whom?, to what?,* or *for what?* after an action verb.

- A sentence may have one, two, or more indirect objects:

  Sara gave Josh the report. (Indirect object is *Josh*; direct object is *report.*)

  Mischa sent Jim and Hannah birthday cards. (Indirect objects are *Jim* and *Hannah*; direct object is *cards.*)

Be careful not to mistake adverbs or objects of prepositional phrases for direct or indirect objects.

3.11 Sharing Traits

Although dolphins and bats do not seem to have much in common, they share a very special ability. What is this ability?

   To answer the question, read each sentence below and determine whether the underlined word is a direct object. If the word is a direct object, write the letter for "yes" in the space above its sentence number at the bottom of the page. If the word is not a direct object, write the letter for "no."

1. Dolphins and bats are both <u>mammals</u>.
   E. Yes   A. No

2. Sailors tell many interesting <u>stories</u> about dolphins.
   N. Yes   S. No

3. Some stories speak of <u>dolphins</u> saving shipwrecked seamen.
   K. Yes   T. No

4. Many people look on <u>dolphins</u> as noble creatures.
   R. Yes   L. No

5. Most bats are <u>active</u> during the night.
   U. Yes   H. No

6. The sudden appearance of a bat in the night startles most <u>people</u>.
   E. Yes   F. No

7. Dolphins and bats share some important <u>traits</u>.
   I. Yes   R. No

8. Like bats, dolphins breathe <u>oxygen</u> from the air.
   C. Yes   E. No

9. Also like bats, dolphins are <u>warm-blooded</u>.
   U. Yes   O. No

___ ___ ___ ___ ___ ___ ___ ___ ___ ___ ___ ___
 6   8   5   9   4   9   8   1   3   7   9   2

Verbs

3.12 Fish Story

There are over twenty thousand species of fish in the world. What are scientists who study fish called?

To answer the question, find the direct object in each sentence below. In the parentheses that follow each sentence, a letter is called for. Find this letter in the direct object, then write the letter in the space above the direct object's sentence number at the bottom of the page. The second one is done for you.

1. Justin's teacher assigned a report for science. (sixth letter)

2. Justin chose the subje**c**t of fish for his report. (sixth letter)

3. The subject required much research. (third letter)

4. Justin searched the Internet for information. (first letter)

5. He also checked numerous books in the library. (second letter)

6. He spent several hours on research. (first letter)

7. He included many excellent details in his report. (sixth letter)

8. He revised the summary of his report after dinner. (seventh letter)

9. His report received the highest grade in the class. (first letter)

__	C	__	__	__	__	__	__	__	__	__	__	__	__
4	2	6	1	6	8	5	7	5	9	4	3	1	3

Verbs

3.13 Iron Ships

During the Civil War, the first battle between ironclad ships took place on March 9, 1862. The North's ship was the USS *Monitor*. What was the original name of the South's ship?

To answer the question, read each sentence below and determine whether the underlined word is an indirect object. If the word is an indirect object, write the letter for "yes" in the space above its sentence number at the bottom of the page. If the word is not an indirect object, write the letter for "no."

1. Cara recently studied the <u>American</u> Civil War in her history class.
   T. Yes   A. No

2. Mrs. Brown, her teacher, showed the <u>class</u> a film about the causes of the war.
   R. Yes   O. No

3. Mrs. Brown taught the <u>students</u> many interesting facts.
   I. Yes   E. No

4. Cara enjoys <u>learning</u> about great events of the past.
   D. Yes   C. No

5. Mrs. Brown gave the <u>class</u> a homework assignment.
   E. Yes   H. No

6. The assignment included a <u>summary</u> of the causes of the war.
   P. Yes   M. No

7. Cara completed the <u>assignment</u> easily.
   N. Yes   K. No

8. The next day Cara handed <u>Mrs. Brown</u> her assignment.
   M. Yes   T. No

9. That evening Cara checked historical <u>websites</u> for information about the Civil War.
   M. Yes   R. No

___ ___ ___ ___ ___ ___ ___ ___ ___
 8   5   2   9   3   6   1   4   7

Verbs

3.14 Miniature Golf

Most Americans are familiar with miniature golf. It is an enjoyable game based on real golf. What was a common early name for miniature golf?

   To answer the question, find the indirect object in each sentence below. In the parentheses that follow each sentence, a letter is called for. Find this letter in the indirect object, then write the letter in the space above the indirect object's sentence number at the bottom of the page. The first one is done for you. You will need to divide the letters into words.

1. Gil handed Ro**b**erto the golf club. (third letter)

2. Gil taught him skills for playing golf. (third letter)

3. Just before starting the game, Gil gave his friend a final tip. (first letter)

4. Roberto offered his instructor a confident smile. (sixth letter)

5. Gil tossed Roberto the ball. (second letter)

6. Roberto gave the ball a solid whack with the club. (third letter)

7. Gil showed his humbled student the proper form. (second letter)

8. Roberto's next shot gave Gil hope. (first letter)

9. At the end of the day Gil bought them lunch. (second letter)

__	__	__	__	__	__	__	B	__	__	__	__
7	5	2	7	9	4	2	1	8	5	6	3

Verbs

3.15 Important Invention

In 1903, Mary Anderson invented something no car should be without. What did she invent?

To answer the question, read each sentence below. Decide whether the underlined word is a direct object, an indirect object, or neither. Write the letter of your answer in the space above its sentence number at the bottom of the page. You will need to divide the letters into words.

1. The invention of the automobile revolutionized transportation around the world.
   T. Direct object   E. Indirect object   H. Neither

2. Several inventors built early models of automobiles in the 1890s.
   L. Direct object   A. Indirect object   U. Neither

3. The inventors proudly showed people their inventions.
   M. Direct object   N. Indirect object   C. Neither

4. Henry Ford produced his first experimental car in 1893.
   N. Direct object   D. Indirect object   S. Neither

5. Automobiles offered people great freedom.
   D. Direct object   P. Indirect object   S. Neither

6. People traveled easily throughout the entire country.
   A. Direct object   Y. Indirect object   E. Neither

7. Today many families own two vehicles.
   D. Direct object   S. Indirect object   U. Neither

8. Lori's parents bought her a car for her eighteenth birthday.
   E. Direct object   R. Indirect object   L. Neither

9. Lori quickly told her friends the news.
   H. Direct object   W. Indirect object   M. Neither

10. Lori loves her new car immensely.
    I. Direct object   E. Indirect object   L. Neither

___ ___ ___ ___ ___ ___ ___ ___ ___ ___ ___ ___ ___ ___ ___
9 10 3   7   4   1 10   6   2   7   9 10   5   6   8   4

Predicate Nominatives and Predicate Adjectives

Predicate nominatives and *predicate adjectives* follow linking verbs. Here are facts about and examples of predicate nominatives:

- A predicate nominative is a noun or pronoun.

- A predicate nominative renames or identifies the subject of a sentence.

- A sentence may have a compound (more than one) predicate nominative.

  Jill is a <u>teacher</u> at a middle school. (*Teacher* identifies *Jill.*)

  The main ingredients are <u>sugar</u> and <u>flour</u>. (*Sugar* and *flour* are names for *ingredients.*)

Here are facts about and examples of predicate adjectives:

- A predicate adjective is an adjective.

- A predicate adjective describes the subject of a sentence.

- A sentence may have a compound predicate adjective.

  The mountain is <u>immense</u>. (*Immense* describes *mountain.*)

  The guide was <u>young</u> and <u>handsome</u>. (*Young* and *handsome* describe the *guide.*)

3.16 The White House

This president was the first president to live in the White House. Who was he?
  To answer the question, decide whether the underlined word in each sentence below is a predicate nominative. If the word is a predicate nomina-tive, write the letter for "yes" in the space above the word's sentence number at the bottom of the page. If the word is not a predicate nominative, write the letter for "no." You will need to divide the letters into words.

1. The White House is the official <u>residence</u> of U.S. presidents.
   A. Yes   R. No

2. The White House is located in <u>Washington, D.C.</u>
   N. Yes   S. No

3. James Hoban was the <u>architect</u> of the White House.
   O. Yes   A. No

4. In the opinion of many people, the White House is <u>magnificent</u>.
   E. Yes   N. No

5. The building is a <u>symbol</u> of our great nation.
   J. Yes   A. No

6. During the War of 1812, the British set <u>fire</u> to the White House.
   E. Yes   M. No

7. White paint was used to <u>cover</u> the smoke-stained exterior walls.
   E. Yes   A. No

8. The "White House" became the official <u>name</u> of the president's home in 1902.
   H. Yes   M. No

9. The White House remains the <u>home</u> of our nation's leader.
   D. Yes   J. No

___ ___ ___ ___ ___ ___ ___ ___ ___
 5   3   8   4   1   9   7   6   2

3.17 Home of the Gods

According to Greek mythology, the gods could be found here. What was the name of this place?

To answer the question, decide whether the underlined word in each sentence below is a predicate adjective. If the word is a predicate adjective, write the letter for "yes" in the space above the word's sentence number at the bottom of the page. If the word is not a predicate adjective, write the letter for "no." You will need to divide the letters into words.

1. Greek mythology is a favorite <u>subject</u> for Tia.
   R. Yes   L. No

2. She loves reading <u>stories</u> of heroes, gods, and fantastic creatures.
   M. Yes   T. No

3. Each story is <u>fascinating</u> to her.
   U. Yes   I. No

4. The stories of Hercules are <u>extraordinary</u>.
   U. Yes   E. No

5. Of all the heroes in Greek myths, Hercules was the <u>greatest</u>.
   S. Yes   D. No

6. Many of the heroes routinely performed <u>spectacular</u> deeds.
   T. Yes   N. No

7. Another of Tia's favorites is the <u>story</u> of Jason and the Argonauts.
   I. Yes   Y. No

8. Jason and his men sailed off in <u>search</u> of a golden fleece.
   P. Yes   M. No

9. Jason was <u>courageous</u> during the quest for the fleece.
   P. Yes   R. No

10. After great adventures the Argonauts were <u>successful</u>.
    O. Yes   E. No

__ __ __ __ __ __ __ __ __ __ __ __
8 10 3 6 2 10 1 7 8 9 4 5

Verbs

3.18 Magical Land

J. M. Barrie wrote the original story of Peter Pan. What were Barrie's first and middle names?

To answer the question, read each sentence below. If the underlined word is a predicate nominative, write the letter for "predicate nominative" in the space above its sentence number at the bottom of the page. If the underlined word is a predicate adjective, write the letter for "predicate adjective." The first letter is provided. You will need to divide the letters into words.

1. The imagination of J. M. Barrie was <u>incredible</u>.
   D. Predicate nominative   S. Predicate adjective

2. Peter Pan is the <u>hero</u> of Barrie's story.
   H. Predicate nominative   N. Predicate adjective

3. The story is a <u>fantasy</u> for people of all ages, especially children.
   W. Predicate nominative   S. Predicate adjective

4. Captain Hook, a cruel pirate, was the <u>villain</u> in the story.
   E. Predicate nominative   G. Predicate adjective

5. Of all the characters in the story, Hook was <u>frightening</u> to young children.
   N. Predicate nominative   M. Predicate adjective

6. Tinker Bell, the fairy, was <u>mischievous</u>.
   H. Predicate nominative   T. Predicate adjective

7. The story is <u>wonderful</u>, a fantastic tale of adventure.
   J. Predicate nominative   A. Predicate adjective

J __ __ __ __ __ __ __ __ __ __ __
   7 5 4 1 5 7 6 6 2 4 3

Verbs

3.19 Starry Night

When ancient astronomers looked at groups of stars in the night sky, they imagined they saw pictures. If you know where to look, and use your imagination, you can see these pictures today. What are these starry pictures called?

To answer the question, match the contraction on the left with the words from which it is formed on the right. Write the letter of your answer in the space above the contraction's number at the bottom of the page.

Contractions	Words
1. could've	O. is not
2. she'll	E. will not
3. isn't	L. was not
4. weren't	H. do not
5. that's	N. does not
6. don't	T. would have
7. won't	A. could have
8. doesn't	S. were not
9. wasn't	C. that is
10. would've	I. she will

___ ___ ___ ___ ___ ___ ___ ___ ___ ___ ___ ___ ___ ___ ___ ___
10   6   7   5   3   8   4   10   7   9   9   1   10   2   3   8   4

Verbs

Verb Tenses

The tense of a verb indicates time. Tense shows when something in a sentence happens, happened, or will happen. The most commonly used tenses of verbs follow.

- The *present tense* expresses current action or state of being.

  They <u>walk</u> for exercise each day.

- The *past tense* expresses action or state of being that has happened.

  They <u>walked</u> yesterday.

- The *future tense* expresses action or state of being that will happen in the future. It is formed by adding the helping verbs *will* or *shall* to the present tense form of the verb.

  They <u>will walk</u> tonight.

- *Present perfect tense* expresses action or state of being that began in the past and that may still be going on. It is formed with the helping verb *has* or *have* and the past participle form of the verb.

  They <u>have walked</u> this morning.

- *Past perfect tense* expresses a past action or state of being that happened before another past action or state of being. It is formed with the helping verb *had* and the past participle.

  They <u>had walked</u> before going to work.

- *Future perfect tense* expresses an action or state of being that will have ended before a specific time or event in the future. It is formed with the helping verbs *will have* or *shall have* and the past participle.

  They <u>will have walked</u> before dinner.

3.20 A First in Space

In March of 1965, this Russian cosmonaut left his spacecraft and accomplished the first "walk" in space. Who was he?

   To answer the question, read each sentence below and decide whether the underlined verb expresses the past, present, or future tense. Write the letter of each answer in the space above its sentence number at the bottom of the page.

1. James <u>learned</u> about the space program in his science class.
   X. Past   K. Present   M. Future

2. The solar system <u>is</u> one of his favorite subjects.
   L. Past   N. Present   H. Future

3. Before retiring, James's grandfather <u>was</u> an astronomer at a nearby university.
   V. Past   S. Present   D. Future

4. James <u>will go</u> to a space museum with his grandfather on Saturday.
   O. Past   H. Present   L. Future

5. They <u>plan</u> to visit all of the exhibits.
   I. Past   L. Present   N. Future

6. James <u>dreams</u> of becoming an astronomer or an astronaut someday.
   T. Past   A. Present   J. Future

7. James <u>will reach</u> his goals through study and hard work.
   Y. Past   S. Present   I. Future

8. James <u>enjoyed</u> the trip to the museum with his grandfather.
   O. Past   I. Present   E. Future

9. His grandfather surely <u>will teach</u> him much about the planets and stars.
   R. Past   U. Present   E. Future

___ ___ ___ ___ ___ ___   ___ ___ ___ ___ ___ ___
 6   4   9   1   9   7   5   9   8   2   8   3

Verbs

3.21 Patriotic Woman

Most students are familiar with Molly Pitcher. During the Battle of Monmouth, she carried pitchers of water to her husband and other soldiers. Molly Pitcher was not this patriot's real name. What was Molly Pitcher's real married name?

To answer the question, find the verb in each of the sentences below and identify its tense. Six tenses follow the sentences. Match the tense of each verb with the letter of its tense. Write the letter in the space above the verb's sentence number at the bottom of the page. You will need to divide the letters into words.

1. Molly Pitcher's maiden name was Ludwig.

2. She is a famous heroine of the American Revolution.

3. Most students and American adults know the name of Molly Pitcher.

4. Taylor's class will do a report on a topic of the Revolutionary War.

5. Mr. Smith had assigned the report before the spring break.

6. Some students waited until after the break to start their research.

7. Taylor has finished her report on Molly Pitcher.

8. By the end of the week all students will have completed their reports.

Answers

Y. Present tense   M. Present perfect tense
A. Past tense   R. Past perfect tense
H. Future tense   S. Future perfect tense

___   ___   ___   ___   ___   ___   ___   ___
 7   6   5   3   4   1   2   8

Verbs

Regular and Irregular Verbs

The basic forms of a verb are called its *principal parts*. These parts are the present, past, the past participle, and the present participle.

Most verbs are known as *regular verbs*. They form their past and past participle forms by adding -*d* or -*ed* to the present form. The past participle requires the helping verbs *have*, *has*, or *had*. Regular verbs form their present participle by adding -*ing*. The present participle requires a form of the verb *be* as a helping verb.

Some regular verbs have minor spelling changes when adding -*d*, -*ed*, or -*ing*. A final -*e* may be dropped (for example, glide, glided, gliding). A consonant may be doubled (grip, gripped, gripping). A -*y* may be changed to -*i* (carry, carried, carrying). Here are some examples of the principal parts of regular verbs:

Present	Past	Past Participle	Present Participle
walk	walked	(have) walked	(are) walking
hike	hiked	(have) hiked	(are) hiking
sip	sipped	(have) sipped	(are) sipping
cry	cried	(have) cried	(are) crying

Not all verbs form their principal parts in these patterns. The past and past participle forms of *irregular verbs* do not end in -*d* or -*ed*. They may change their spelling, or they may not change at all. Here are some examples:

Present	Past	Past Participle	Present Participle
begin	began	(have) begun	(are) beginning
come	came	(have) come	(are) coming
give	gave	(have) given	(are) giving
hit	hit	(have) hit	(are) hitting
know	knew	(have) known	(are) knowing
teach	taught	(have) taught	(are) teaching

Learning the forms of irregular verbs will help you to use them correctly.

3.22 Special Eyes

These animals can move their eyes in two different directions at the same time. They are also wonderful at disguising themselves. What are these animals called?

To answer the question, match the present-tense form of the irregular verb on the left with its past-tense form on the right. Write the letter of the past-tense form in the space above the verb's number at the bottom of the page.

Present   **Past**

1. freeze   Z. freezed   A. froze

2. sing   N. sang   E. sung

3. do   N. done   S. did

4. see   H. saw   I. seen

5. begin   U. begun   M. began

6. swim   T. swum   O. swam

7. get   S. gotted   L. got

8. catch   C. caught   L. catched

9. draw   E. drew   R. drawn

10. steal   E. stole   U. stold

___ ___ ___ ___ ___ ___ ___ ___ ___ ___
 8   4   1   5   9   7   10 6   2   3

Verbs

74

3.23 Unusual Creature

Weighing up to two and a half tons and stretching up to fifty-five feet in length, this creature is the largest animal without a backbone on Earth. What is the common name for this animal?

To answer the question, match the present-tense form of the irregular verb on the left with its past-tense form on the right. Write the letter of the past-tense form in the space above the verb's number at the bottom of the page. You will need to divide the letters into words.

Present   **Past**

1. tear   O. torn   N. tore

2. sink   E. sunk   I. sank

3. break   S. broke   K. brake

4. tell   R. toll   T. told

5. throw   I. threw   C. thrown

6. come   S. come   D. came

7. wear   A. wore   T. worn

8. bring   G. brought   O. brang

9. shut   Q. shut   E. shutted

10. sit   M. set   U. sat

___ ___ ___ ___ ___ ___ ___ ___ ___ ___
 8   5   7   1   4   3   9   10   2   6

Verbs

3.24 Out of This World

In 1962, this astronaut was the first American to orbit the Earth. Who was this person?

To answer the question, complete each sentence below with the correct form of the irregular verb. Choose your answers from the verbs that follow the sentence. Write the letter of each answer in the space above its sentence number at the bottom of the page. You will need to divide the letters into words.

1. After school yesterday Alison's mother _____ her to the library.
   N. drove   L. drived

2. Alison _____ out several books on space.
   E. taked   N. took

3. She _____ at the checkout counter for several minutes.
   G. stood   D. standed

4. She _____ many of her classmates there.
   P. seen   J. saw

5. Mrs. Walters, Alison's science teacher, _____ the students a project on the solar system.
   T. gived   H. gave

6. Students _____ different topics for their projects.
   E. chose   A. choosed

7. Alison _____ the project could raise her science grade.
   O. thought   E. thinked

8. She _____ an excellent picture of the solar system as a part of her project.
   D. drawed   N. drew

9. She also _____ a model of the sun and planets.
   L. made   T. maked

___ ___ ___ ___ ___ ___ ___ ___ ___
 4   7   5   1   3   9   6   2   8

Verbs

3.25 Office Essential

In 1899, a Norwegian invented a product that is found in just about every office. What was this invention?

To answer the question, find the verb in each sentence below. Determine whether the verb is used correctly. If it is correct, write the letter for "correct" in the space above its sentence number at the bottom of the page. If the verb is not used correctly, write the letter for "incorrect." You will need to divide the letters into words.

1. Stacey went with her mother to work on Take Your Daughter to Work Day.
   I. Correct   E. Incorrect

2. They leaved early in the morning to avoid traffic.
   P. Correct   E. Incorrect

3. They begun work at 9:00 A.M.
   N. Correct   S. Incorrect

4. Stacey set in a chair beside her mother's desk.
   O. Correct   A. Incorrect

5. Her mother gave Stacy plenty of work to do.
   R. Correct   T. Incorrect

6. Stacey writ the addresses on packages for clients.
   S. Correct   L. Incorrect

7. She brang the packages to the mail room for her mother.
   E. Correct   P. Incorrect

8. Stacey seen some packages with her mother's name on them.
   M. Correct   P. Incorrect

9. She took the packages back to her mother's office.
   C. Correct   E. Incorrect

10. Stacey and her mother ate lunch in the company's cafeteria.
    P. Correct   C. Incorrect

___ ___ ___ ___ ___ ___ ___ ___ ___ ___
10   4   8   2   5   9   6   1   7   3

Verbs

Agreement Between Subjects and Verbs

Subjects must agree with their verbs in number.

- A singular subject requires the singular form of a verb. A plural subject requires the plural form of a verb. Because the singular and plural forms of verbs in the past tense (except for the verb *be*) are the same, most confusion with agreement occurs with verbs in the present tense.

   Nan plays basketball on the middle school team. (present)

   The Williams twins play baseball on the middle school team. (present)

   Nan played basketball on the middle school team. (past)

   The Williams twins played baseball on the middle school team. (past)

- Compound subjects (whether singular or plural) that are joined by *and* require the plural form of the verb.

   Beth and Maria ride the bus to school.

   The Taylors and the Smiths live on the same street.

- When the parts of a compound subject are joined by *or* or *nor,* the verb agrees with the nearest subject.

   Valerie or Billy is in change of the pep rally. (*Billy* agrees with *is.*)

   His parents or Tom has the keys. (*Tom* agrees with *has.*)

   Neither Larissa nor her parents have the directions. (*Parents* agree with *have.*)

- Prepositional phrases that come between subjects and verbs do not affect agreement.

   The crickets in the field chirp all night. (The prepositional phrase is *in the field.*)

- The pronouns *I* and *you* require the plural forms of verbs in the present tense.

   I play saxophone in the school band.

   You play drums in the school band.

   The brothers play drums in the school band.

3.26 Old Writing

The Maya were one of the most advanced of all the Native American groups. They invented a form of writing that used pictures to represent sounds. What are these pictures called?

To answer the question, complete each sentence below by writing the correct present-tense form of the verb. Choose your answers from the verbs following each sentence. Write the letter of each answer in the space above its sentence number at the bottom of the page.

1. The meeting of the history club _____ at 3:15 today.
   E. begin   O. begins

2. Students _____ for books on history in the library.
   U. looks   Y. look

3. Carly _____ history to be fascinating.
   E. finds   P. find

4. She and Jason _____ to the history club in school.
   T. belongs   P. belong

5. Many students _____ members of the club.
   I. are   M. is

6. Sara _____ learning about prehistoric cultures.
   R. enjoys   S. enjoy

7. Anna _____ to attend a lecture about ancient Mayan culture.
   G. plans   C. plan

8. Jason and his brother _____ archeology is an interesting subject.
   S. thinks   H. think

9. Sue _____ the Maya had the most advanced culture in the Americas.
   S. believes   C. believe

10. Raymondo _____ to read about the history of the Far East.
    T. like   L. likes

___ ___ ___ ___ ___ ___ ___ ___ ___ ___ ___
 8   5   3   6   1   7 10   2   4   8   9

Verbs

3.27 Time to Wake Up

This New Hampshire man invented the first alarm clock in 1787. What was his name?

To answer the question, complete each sentence below by writing the correct present-tense form of the verb. Choose your answers from the verbs following each sentence. Write the letter of each answer in the space above its sentence number at the bottom of the page.

1. Scott _____ the buzz of his alarm clock to be the worst sound in the world.

   M. consider   T. considers

2. He _____ sleeping late in the morning.

   E. loves   A. love

3. On weekdays, his alarm clock _____ off at 7:00 A.M.

   S. go   C. goes

4. The other members of his family _____ up early every morning without an alarm clock.

   E. wakes   N. wake

5. His little sisters, Sara and Suzanne, _____ him each morning with their boundless energy.

   S. astonish   Y. astonishes

6. They _____ downstairs right after their parents.

   U. scamper   O. scampers

7. After breakfast Scott usually _____ fully alert.

   J. are   L. is

8. Neither Sara nor Suzanne _____ the reason for his sleepiness in the morning.

   R. understand   H. understands

9. Scott _____ the reason.

   V. knows   K. know

10. He of all the family members _____ up too late at night.

    E. stay   I. stays

___ ___ ___ ___   ___ ___ ___ ___ ___ ___ ___ ___
 7   2   9   10   8   6   1   3   8   10   4   5

3.28 Tasty Treat

In 1874, Robert Green created this tasty treat. What treat did he create?

To answer the question, complete each sentence below by writing the correct present-tense form of the verb. Choose your answers from the verbs after each sentence. Write the letter of each answer in the space above its sentence number at the bottom of the page. You will need to divide the letters into words.

1. Jasmine's uncle Tyler _____ a candy shop.
   S. owns   N. own

2. Her uncle _____ an excellent businessperson.
   R. is   S. are

3. There _____ hundreds of different kinds of candy in his shop.
   C. is   M. are

4. Either Jasmine or one of her brothers _____ in the shop every Saturday.
   O. helps   E. help

5. She or her brothers usually _____ in the afternoon.
   I. works   A. work

6. Last Saturday there _____ a lot to do.
   E. was   C. were

7. Uncle Tyler always _____ his niece and nephews for their help.
   I. thank   D. thanks

8. Jasmine _____ about owning a candy shop herself someday.
   P. think   I. thinks

9. Neither her parents nor her uncle _____ of her secret ambition.
   I. know   C. knows

___ ___ ___ ___ ___ ___ ___ ___ ___ ___ ___ ___
 8   9   6   9   2   6   5   3   1   4   7   5

Verbs

3.29 Famous Cartoon Character

Along with Mickey Mouse and Donald Duck, Goofy is one of Disney's most famous characters. But this cartoon star was not always known as Goofy. What was Goofy's original name?

   To answer the question, read the sentences below and identify the verbs. Determine whether each verb agrees with its subject. If the verb agrees with its subject, write the letter for "yes" in the space above its sentence number. If the verb does not agree with its subject, write the letter for "no."

1. Countless children and adults watch cartoons.
   I. Yes   E. No

2. Some cartoon characters is as popular as real Hollywood movie stars.
   Y. Yes   W. No

3. Tess and some of her friends in seventh grade are experts on the history of cartoons and animation.
   A. Yes   E. No

4. The first animated cartoons was created nearly a hundred years ago.
   N. Yes   Y. No

5. Margo, one of Tess's sisters, admire early animators.
   S. Yes   G. No

6. The work of these first animators were slow and painstaking.
   T. Yes   P. No

7. The girls share a big collection containing several old cartoons on DVD.
   P. Yes   I. No

8. Sometimes they have a cartoon party with their friends.
   D. Yes   T. No

9. Friends of Tess and Margo comes to their house to watch classic cartoons.
   M. Yes   D. No

____ ____ ____ ____ ____   ____ ____ ____ ____
 8   1   6   7   4   9   3   2   5

Verbs

3.30 First Vaccine

In 1796, Dr. Edward Jenner developed the first successful vaccine. What disease did this vaccine prevent?

To answer the question, read the paragraph below. Determine whether the underlined words are verbs or verb phrases. Also determine whether they are used correctly. Starting with the first sentence, write the letter beneath each correct verb or verb phrase in order on the blanks at the bottom of the page.

Edward Jenner <u>was</u> a British physician. He <u>was born on</u> May 17, 1749. Always
        S   I

<u>curious</u> about nature, he <u>became a keen</u> observer of the world. This trait <u>would help</u>
N   F   M

him in his research. In Jenner's time, doctors <u>had</u> few medicines <u>for treating</u> serious
                                 A   T

diseases. Many of these diseases <u>resulted</u> in death. After studying medicine for
                                L

<u>several</u> years, Jenner <u>started</u> a medical practice. Hoping <u>to prevent</u> one of the most
U   L   E

serious diseases of his day, he <u>developed</u> procedures for vaccinating people. His
                           P

methods <u>were</u> successful. Jenner <u>did not fully</u> understand his discovery. About
        O   R

seventy-five years later, the French chemist Louis Pasteur <u>would use</u> Jenner's early
                                         X

work as a basis for his own experiments with vaccines. Today, vaccines <u>protect us</u>
                                         M

from many serious diseases.

___ ___ ___ ___ ___ ___ ___ ___

Verbs

3.31 Great Inventor

With a record 1,093 U.S. patents to his credit, this man ranks among the greatest inventors of all time. Who was he?

To answer the question, read each sentence below and identify its verb or verb phrase. If the verb or verb phrase is used correctly, write the letter for "correct" in the space above its sentence number at the bottom of the page. If for any reason the verb or verb phrase is used incorrectly, write the letter for "incorrect." You will need to divide the letters into words.

1. Most inventors can be described as curious people.
   E. Correct   C. Incorrect

2. The goal of most inventors are to make life better or easier.
   R. Correct   A. Incorrect

3. Inventors usually has a talent for looking at problems in creative ways.
   S. Correct   N. Incorrect

4. Most successful inventions are the result of hard work and dedication.
   M. Correct   D. Incorrect

5. Sometimes luck or a mistake play a part in developing an invention.
   F. Correct   T. Incorrect

6. Creative men and women have been inventing tools and machines throughout history.
   I. Correct   U. Incorrect

7. The invention of wheels over five thousand years ago were a major advance.
   R. Correct   H. Incorrect

8. The electric light, gasoline motor, and automobile were other important inventions.
   D. Correct   M. Incorrect

9. Certainly the invention of the airplane has changed the world.
   O. Correct   E. Incorrect

10. The invention of computers have helped bring about the Information Age.
    I. Correct   S. Incorrect

___ ___ ___ ___ ___ ___ ___ ___ ___ ___ ___ ___
 5   7   9   4   2   10   1   8   6   10   9   3

Verbs

3.32 High Point in Europe

At an elevation of 15,770 feet, this mountain in France and Italy is the highest in Europe. What is its name?

To answer the question, read each sentence below and identify the under-lined word or phrase. Match the word or phrase with the term that best describes it. Choose your answers from the terms that follow the sentences. Write the letter of each answer in the space above its sentence number at the bottom of the page.

1. Europe is the second smallest continent in the world.

2. The Alps, Europe's highest mountains, offer the world much beauty.

3. Rising over fifteen thousand feet above sea level, the Alps are majestic.

4. In the past much of Europe was covered with thick forests.

5. Today the continent is home to many countries, cities, and towns.

6. During the fifteenth and sixteenth centuries, Europeans explored much of the world.

7. Thousands of people from Europe went to the New World in hopes of starting new lives.

8. Many Americans trace their roots to Europe.

Answers

Y. Present tense   M. Present perfect tense
B. Action verb   N. Predicate nominative
A. Linking verb   C. Predicate adjective
M. Irregular verb   L. Direct object
T. Verb phrase   O. Indirect object

___ ___ ___ ___ ___ ___ ___ ___ ___
 7   2   5   4   6   8   1   5   3

Verbs

Pronouns

Pronouns are words that replace nouns. There are many different kinds of pronouns that serve a variety of purposes in sentences.

The tip sheets and worksheets that follow address the different pronouns and their usage. The first tip sheet introduces pronouns, and Worksheets 4.1 through 4.4 concentrate on identifying pronouns and antecedents. The next two tip sheets and Worksheets 4.5 through 4.9 cover subject and object pronouns. The fourth tip sheet and Worksheet 4.10 concentrate on who and whom. The next tip sheet and Worksheets 4.11 through 4.13 focus on possessive pronouns, while Worksheet 4.14 addresses pronoun contractions. Worksheets 4.15 and 4.16 cover indefinite pronouns, and Worksheets 4.17 through 4.19 conclude the section with reviews.

TIP SHEET

Pronouns

Pronouns are words that take the place of nouns. The noun that a pronoun refers to is called its *antecedent*. The most important kinds of pronouns follow.

- *Personal pronouns* usually refer to people but may also refer to places, things, or ideas. They may be singular or plural.

	Singular	Plural
First person	I, me	we, us
Second person	you	you
Third person	he, she, him, her, it	they, them

- *Possessive pronouns* are personal pronouns that show *who* or *what* owns something. They may be singular or plural.

	Singular	Plural
First person	my, mine	our, ours
Second person	your, yours	your, yours
Third person	his, her, hers, its	their, theirs

- *Indefinite pronouns* are pronouns that do not refer to specific persons, places, things, or ideas. Most indefinite pronouns are singular. Some are plural. Some are singular or plural depending on their use in a sentence. Following are some examples:

Singular	Plural	Singular or Plural
anybody, everybody, no one	both	all
anyone, everyone, nothing	few	any
anything, everything, somebody	many	most
each, neither, someone	several	none
either, nobody, something	others	some

- *Demonstrative pronouns* are the words *this, that, these,* and *those.* Demonstrative pronouns point out their antecedents.

- *Reflexive pronouns* end in *self* or *selves.* Reflexive pronouns refer back to the nouns or pronouns used earlier in a sentence.

- *Interrogative pronouns* are used in questions: *who, whose, whom, which,* and *what.*

88

© Gary Robert Muschla

4.1 Long-Distance Speedster

Capable of reaching speeds of seventy miles per hour, the cheetah is the fastest land animal over short distances. Able to run up to thirty-five miles per hour for up to four miles, this is the fastest land animal over long distances. What is the name of this animal?

To answer the question, find the pronoun in each set of words below. Write the letter of the pronoun in the space above its line number at the bottom of the page.

1. U. notice	H. they	E. am	R. nightfall
2. M. as	B. landscape	V. chilly	T. mine
3. D. evening	E. severe	L. her	O. rapidly
4. S. common	W. to	N. kennel	G. you
5. A. their	I. equipment	U. is	C. language
6. H. author	R. us	T. unusual	N. dusk
7. W. at	E. wanted	X. natural	P. its
8. L. spoken	E. your	Y. amusing	S. for
9. I. not	M. third	O. our	R. do
10. N. I	R. lonely	E. magazine	B. there

___ ___ ___ ___ ___ ___ ___ ___ ___   ___ ___ ___ ___ ___ ___ ___ ___
 7   6   9 10   4   1   9   6 10   5 10   2   8   3   9   7   8

4.2 Ancient Scientist

This ancient Greek scholar was a noted mathematician. But he was also one of the world's first true scientists because he tested his ideas with experiments. Who was he?

To answer the question, find the pronoun in each set of words below. Write the letter of the pronoun in the space above its line number at the bottom of the page.

1. U. an	R. emergency	I. left	E. anybody
2. I. herself	C. machine	H. like	S. of
3. N. complete	F. than	H. this	M. before
4. A. sell	E. nothing	I. definite	S. in
5. P. celebration	W. calling	V. depend	R. we
6. D. everyone	Y. place	L. correct	A. enormously
7. E. according	A. it	O. volunteer	S. on
8. S. who	D. to	E. record	M. treasure
9. H. at	O. uniform	J. scenery	C. our
10. R. an	F. indicate	M. whose	T. after

___ ___ ___ ___ ___ ___ ___ ___ ___ ___
7   5   9   3   2   10   1   6   4   8

Pronouns

4.3 Strike Up the Band!

Because of the patriotic marching songs this band leader and composer wrote, he became known as the March King. Who was he?

To answer the question, find the pronoun in each sentence below. Only one pronoun is underlined in each sentence. Write the letter of the pronoun in the space above its sentence number at the bottom of the page. You will need to divide the letters into words.

1. Carly, Tom, and their parents enjoy the music of marching bands.
                  N   E   M   R

2. They find marching music to be energizing.
    U I   N   D

3. Carly does not realize her feet are tapping along with the beat.
              R   A   S   B

4. She and Tom are members of the school band.
    L O   C   T

5. Just about everyone in the school likes listening to the band.
       N   P   H   S

6. The band at our school is small.
    H   A   O   E

7. The size of a band is not as important as the abilities of its members.
      Y   E   O   I

8. Are you a member of the band?
    T J   G   R

9. Jessica and I are planning to join the band next year.
       O H   E   M

10. To do well, we must practice every day.
       P E S   R

___ ___ ___ ___ ___ ___ ___ ___ ___ ___ ___ ___ ___ ___ ___
8   6   9   1   5   9   7   4   7   5   10   6   2   10   3

4.4 Medical Breakthrough

In the mid 1860s this doctor was the first to use an antiseptic to prevent infections during surgery. Who was he?

To answer the question, read each sentence below. Find the antecedent of the underlined pronoun. In the parentheses after the sentence, a letter is called for. Find this letter in the antecedent, then write the letter in the space above its sentence number at the bottom of the page. The first one is done for you. You will need to divide the letters into words.

1. The children in the Warren family often joke that they are accident prone. (second letter)

2. When Robbie cut his finger yesterday, his mother put antiseptic on it. (second letter)

3. As his mother cleaned the cut, she explained that the antiseptic would prevent infection. (third letter)

4. Robbie was glad that he would not have to go to the doctor. (second letter)

5. Robbie's sister Jenna recalled when she broke her ankle while playing soccer. (first letter)

6. For the next few weeks, Robbie helped his sister with her crutches. (sixth letter)

7. Pixie, the family's pet poodle, sprained her ankle once. (first letter)

8. Cutie, the family's kitten, seemed to smile to himself as Pixie limped around the house for a few days. (fifth letter)

9. But the poodle seemed to smile when she got more attention than the cat. (fifth letter)

10. The family members promise that they will try to avoid accidents in the future. (seventh letter)

__ __ __ __ __ H __ __ __ __ __ __
5   4   10 8   7   1   9   2   10 3   8   6

Subject and Object Pronouns

Pronouns can be used in different ways in sentences. They are often used as subjects or objects.

- *Subject pronouns* (also known as pronouns in the nominative case) are used as subjects or predicate nominatives in sentences. The subject pronouns are *I, you, he, she, it, we, they, who,* and *whoever.*

  I played video games last night. (subject)

  They went to the movies. (subject)

  Who went to the game? (subject)

  This is he. (predicate nominative)

  The students were Margo and she. (predicate nominative)

- *Object pronouns* (also known as pronouns in the objective case) are used as direct objects, indirect objects, and objects of prepositions. The object pronouns are *me, you, him, her, it, us, them, whom,* and *whomever.*

  Tom called her yesterday. (direct object)

  Whom did Jason contact? (direct object)

  Mia sent them the package. (indirect object)

  Do these keys belong to him? (object of the preposition *to*)

4.5 Far Below Sea Level

With its surface 1,349 feet below sea level, this is the lowest lake in the world. What is its name?

To answer the question, read the story below. Determine whether the underlined pronouns are subject pronouns. Starting with the first sentence, write the letters beneath the subject pronouns in order on the blanks at the bottom of the page. You will need to divide the letters into words.

Amy, Melissa, and William met in <u>their</u> school's library. <u>They</u> were working
                                         G   D

together on a science project. After the librarian gave <u>them</u> some reference books, the
                                                         R

students started searching for possible ideas.

"<u>We</u> need a good topic," Amy said to <u>her</u> friends.
 E   I

<u>They</u> began to brainstorm, but couldn't decide on a subject.
 A

"Can <u>you</u> look in here?" said Melissa to William, handing <u>him</u> a book.
     D   R

"How about the water cycle?" <u>he</u> said.
                                S

"That topic sounds good to <u>me</u>," said Amy.
                            N

"There should be enough information for <u>us</u>," said Melissa.
                                          T

"<u>Who</u> wants to check for information on the Internet?" said Amy.
   E

"I will," said Melissa, giving <u>them</u> a big smile.
 A   N

The students began <u>their</u> research.
                     R

____ ____ ____ ____ ____ ____ ____ ____

4.6 Speedy Bird

Although this bird cannot fly, it can run up to forty miles per hour. What is the name of this fast-running bird?

To answer the question, read the story below. Determine whether the underlined pronouns are object pronouns. Starting with the first sentence, write the letters beneath the object pronouns in order on the blanks at the bottom of the page. You will need to reverse the letters.

Kerrie and her older sister Samantha went on a nature walk recently. They took
          S   N

lunch and plenty of equipment with them.
                                   H

"Do you think we will see any animals?" Kerrie asked as they stood in a small
      O   N   U

clearing.

"We might," said Samantha. "Please hand me the binoculars."
  S   C

Kerrie pulled the binoculars from her knapsack and handed them to her. She
                          M   I   A

watched as Samantha scanned the surrounding area.

"There. Do you see it?" Samantha said, pointing at a stand of trees. "A fawn.
        N   R

And there's a bigger deer just behind him."
                                      T

"Yes," said Kerrie. "I see them. But they don't see us."
            O   S   L   O

___ ___ ___ ___ ___ ___ ___

Avoiding Mistakes with Subject and Object Pronouns

To avoid making mistakes when using subject and object pronouns, remember these tips:

- Only the following pronouns can be used as subjects or predicate nominatives: *I, you, he, she, it, we, they, who,* and *whoever.*

- Only the following pronouns can be used as direct objects, indirect objects, or objects of prepositions: *me, you, him, her, it, us, them, whom,* and *whomever.*

- Mistakes often occur when pronouns are a part of compound subjects and objects.

  Bryan and me played basketball yesterday. (incorrect; *me* can be used only as an object)

  Bryan and I played basketball yesterday. (correct)

  Lindsay and her went shopping. (incorrect; *her* is an object)

  Lindsay and she went shopping. (correct)

  Tyrique and them love playing video games. (incorrect; *them* can be used only as an object)

  Tyrique and they love playing video games. (correct)

  Between you and I, I think the soccer team faces a tough season. (incorrect; *I* can be used only as a subject pronoun and cannot be used as the object of the preposition *between*)

  Between you and me, I think the soccer team faces a tough season. (correct)

- To make sure you are using pronouns in compound subjects correctly, read each pronoun separately with the verb. Mistakes will become obvious.

  Bryan and me played basketball yesterday. (incorrect)

  Bryan played basketball yesterday. (correct)

  Me played basketball yesterday. (incorrect)

  I played basketball yesterday. (correct)

  Bryan and I played basketball yesterday. (correct)

4.7 Big Change

These cold-blooded animals usually begin life living in water and breathing with gills. Later they develop lungs and breathe air. What are these kinds of animals called?

To answer the question, read each sentence below. Replace the underlined noun or nouns with the correct pronoun. Choose your answers from the pronouns that follow each sentence. Write the letter of each answer in the space above its sentence number at the bottom of the page.

1. Last week <u>Lisa</u> went camping with her family.
   I. she   S. her

2. <u>Her mother</u> and Lisa drove to the campsite first.
   I. Her   M. She

3. <u>Lisa's brother Billy and her father</u> left a few hours later.
   S. They   R. Them

4. <u>Billy</u> had to play in his baseball team's last game of the season.
   I. He   R. Him

5. Billy and Lisa's father joined <u>Lisa and her mother</u> at the campsite.
   U. they   A. them

6. Once there, the <u>family</u> set up the camp.
   Z. them   P. they

7. The next morning Lisa's mother said to the children, "Come with <u>your father and me</u> to the lake."
   D. they   B. us

8. "<u>Billy and I</u> will see you there in a little while," Lisa said.
   H. We   A. Us

9. Later Lisa sent a card to <u>her Uncle Bob</u>.
   A. him   L. he

10. That afternoon Lisa convinced <u>her mother</u> to go hiking.
    E. she   N. her

___ ___ ___ ___ ___ ___ ___ ___ ___ ___
 9   2   6   8   4   7   1   5   10   3

4.8 Famous Cow

According to some accounts, in 1871 Mrs. O'Leary's cow kicked a lantern and was responsible for this event. What was it?

   To answer the question, complete each sentence below with the correct pronoun. Choose your answers from the pronouns that follow each sentence. Write the letter of each answer in the space above its sentence number at the bottom of the page. You will need to divide the letters into words.

1. Kim and _____ are sisters and best friends.
   A. I   T. me

2. _____ do just about everything together.
   O. We   E. Us

3. _____ is only a year older than I am.
   R. She   E. Her

4. Our friends tell _____ that we are a lot alike.
   C. we   T. us

5. _____ and I like the same music, same sports, and same kinds of books.
   F. She   M. Her

6. We remind _____ that we have our differences, too.
   E. they   G. them

7. Kim's favorite subject is science, but history is the subject for _____.
   O. I   E. me

8. I believe that understanding the past can help _____ make better decisions in the present.
   U. we   H. us

9. _____ does not understand the past will make the same kinds of mistakes.
   I. Whoever   E. Whomever

10. Talking like that probably makes _____ sound like a history teacher.
    L. I   C. me

___ ___ ___ ___ ___ ___ ___ ___ ___ ___ ___ ___ ___ ___
 4   8   7   10   8   9   10   1   6   2   5   9   3   7

4.9 Wizard's Wand

J. K. Rowling is the author of the Harry Potter series. What do the letters J. K. stand for?

To answer the question, read each sentence below. Determine whether the subject and object pronouns are used correctly. If the pronouns in the sentence are used correctly, write the letter for "correct" in the space above the sentence number at the bottom of the page. If at least one of the pronouns is used incorrectly, write the letter for "incorrect." You will need to divide the letters into words. The first letter is provided.

1. My sister Marla and me have read all of the Harry Potter books.
   R. Correct   L. Incorrect

2. Between you and I, I think some of the earlier books are better than the most recent ones.
   Y. Correct   T. Incorrect

3. Marla disagrees with me, and she says that the stories keep getting better and better.
   O. Correct   A. Incorrect

4. I can't think of one person who doesn't like the stories.
   H. Correct   L. Incorrect

5. Karyn borrowed one of the books from me.
   A. Correct   N. Incorrect

6. She invited Marla and I to go with her and her mom to the movies to see the latest story.
   C. Correct   K. Incorrect

7. We went with them on Saturday.
   E. Correct   R. Incorrect

8. Karyn's mom and her picked us up after dinner.
   E. Correct   N. Incorrect

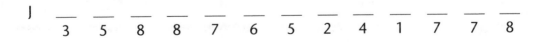

J __ __ __ __ __ __ __ __ __ __ __ __ __
  3 5 8 8 7 6 5 2 4 1 7 7 8

Who and Whom

Use the following tips to help you avoid mistakes with *who* and *whom*.

- *Who* is a subject pronoun.

  <u>Who</u> is going to the movies?

  <u>Who</u> is in your group?

- *Whom* is an object pronoun.

  To <u>whom</u> was the package addressed?

  <u>Whom</u> did you ask?

- There is a simple way to make sure you are using these words correctly. Substitute *he*, *she*, or *they* for *who*. Substitute *him*, *her*, or *them* for *whom*. If *who* or *whom* is used as an interrogative pronoun and asks a question, turn the sentence into a statement. If the substituted pronouns make a correct sentence, you have used *who* or *whom* correctly.

  <u>Who</u> called last night? (correct)   <u>Whom</u> called last night? (incorrect)

  <u>He</u> called last night. (correct)   <u>Him</u> called last night. (incorrect)

  <u>Whom</u> did you call? (correct)   <u>Who</u> did you call? (incorrect)

  You called <u>him</u>. (correct)   You called <u>he</u>. (incorrect)

  <u>Whom</u> was the package for? (correct)   <u>Who</u> was the package for? (incorrect)

  The package was for <u>her</u>. (correct)   The package was for <u>she</u>. (incorrect)

4.10 Designer of Dolls

In 1977, Xavier Roberts designed these dolls to help pay his way through school. What famous dolls did he design?

To answer the question, read each sentence below. If *who* or *whom* is used correctly, write the letter for "correct" in the space above the sentence number at the bottom of the page. If *who* or *whom* is used incorrectly, write the letter for "incorrect." You will need to reverse and divide the letters into words.

1. Who is Xavier Roberts?
   E. Correct   B. Incorrect

2. Who, if anyone, did he work with in designing dolls?
   B. Correct   T. Incorrect

3. Whom would have thought those dolls would become so popular?
   S. Correct   H. Incorrect

4. Do you know anyone who has them?
   G. Correct   D. Incorrect

5. Whom designs new models now?
   A. Correct   P. Incorrect

6. Who did you send one to as a gift?
   E. Correct   A. Incorrect

7. To whom did you address the package?
   C. Correct   K. Incorrect

8. Who finally received the package?
   B. Correct   N. Incorrect

___ ___ ___ ___ ___ ___ ___ ___ ___ ___ ___ ___
 3   7   2   6   5   1   4   6   8   8   6   7

Possessive Pronouns

Possessive pronouns show ownership or possession.

- The following are possessive pronouns: *my, mine, your, yours, his, her, hers, its, our, ours, their, theirs,* and *whose.*

- Some possessive pronouns are used with nouns in sentences: *my, your, her, its, our, their,* and *whose.*

  <u>Your keys</u> are on the table.

  <u>Their house</u> is at the end of the street.

  <u>Whose</u> coat is that?

- Some possessive pronouns are used alone: *mine, yours, hers, ours,* and *theirs.*

  That locker is <u>hers</u>.

  <u>Yours</u> is down the hall.

- The pronoun *his* is commonly used with a noun or alone.

  He lost <u>his history book</u>.

  That history book is <u>his</u>.

- Do not confuse possessive pronouns with pronoun contractions.

Possessive Pronoun	Contraction
your	you're (you are)
its	it's (it is)
their	they're (they are)
whose	who's (who is)

- Remember that possessive pronouns do not have apostrophes. (Possessive nouns have apostrophes.)

4.11 First Ford

Henry Ford built one of the world's first automobiles. What did he call his first car?

To answer the question, find the possessive pronoun in each set of pronouns below. Write the letter of the possessive pronoun in the space above its line number at the bottom of the page.

1. S. me | I. mine | L. somebody | R. you
2. U. it | H. she | T. you | A. ours
3. N. each | D. they | W. him | R. its
4. E. yours | N. us | S. nothing | R. anyone
5. A. nobody | U. hers | E. they're | H. he
6. N. anything | S. we | L. your | C. himself
7. O. whom | H. something | D. my | P. both
8. C. I | M. someone | T. who | Q. their
9. Y. his | K. everybody | S. them | I. it's
10. S. you're | J. all | C. whose | R. nobody

___ ___ ___ ___ ___ ___ ___ ___ ___ ___ ___
8   5   2   7   3   1   10 9   10 6   4

Pronouns

4.12 Long Life

This is one of the few animals in the world that has a longer average life span than people. What is the name of this animal?

To answer the question, complete each sentence below by choosing the correct possessive pronoun. Choose your answers from the pronouns that follow each sentence. Write the letter of each answer in the space above its sentence number at the bottom of the page. You will need to divide the letters into words.

1. My group was preparing for _____ presentation about preserving the environment for wildlife.
   E. our   N. ours

2. I thought that all of the group members had _____ information ready.
   U. their   H. they're

3. "_____ folder is on the table?" I asked.
   K. Who's   O. Whose

4. "That folder is _____," said Maria.
   E. my   L. mine

5. After Maria got her folder, Natalie couldn't find _____.
   R. hers   S. her

6. "_____ folder is on the desk at the back of the room," Tom said to Natalie.
   X. Your   Y. You're

7. Natalie started the presentation with _____ concerns about the environment.
   D. hers   T. her

8. I followed with _____ part of the presentation.
   M. mine   T. my

9. Our first slide was of a lake with _____ blue water.
   T. it's   B. its

__	__	__	__	__	__	__	__	__
9	3	6	8	2	5	7	4	1

4.13 Out in the Wilderness

This wilderness area was established as the first national park in 1872. What is the name of this park?

To answer the question, read the sentences below. Find the possessive pronouns and determine whether they are used correctly. If the possessive pronouns are used correctly, write the letter for "correct" in the space above the sentence number at the bottom of the page. If at least one possessive pronoun in a sentence is used incorrectly, write the letter for "incorrect." You will need to reverse the word.

1. Randy and his family went camping last weekend in one of our country's national parks.

   T. Correct   N. Incorrect

2. They loaded they're gear in the back of the family's van.

   L. Correct   N. Incorrect

3. Randy compared his new knapsack to his sister's old one, and found that his was bigger than hers.

   S. Correct   I. Incorrect

4. She said, "But mine has more compartments."

   W. Correct   R. Incorrect

5. "Who's bag is this?" asked their father.

   D. Correct   O. Incorrect

6. "Its mine," said Randy.

   R. Correct   E. Incorrect

7. "Be sure to get all of you're things," said their father.

   S. Correct   Y. Incorrect

8. "I have all my stuff," said Randy, ready to leave.

   L. Correct   F. Incorrect

___   ___   ___   ___   ___   ___   ___   ___   ___   ___   ___
 6   2   5   1   3   4   5   8   8   6   7

4.14 Towering Volcano

Rising seventeen miles from the surface of the planet, with a crater fifty miles wide, this volcano on Mars is thought to be the biggest in our solar system. What is its name?

To answer the question, match each contraction on the left with the words from which it is formed on the right. Write the letter of your answer in the space above the contraction's number at the bottom of the page.

Contractions	Words
1. you're	P. who is
2. it's	M. you would
3. she'll	O. he would
4. they're	U. you are
5. I'm	N. I have
6. you'd	S. she will
7. they've	Y. we will
8. who's	L. they are
9. he'd	O. it is
10. I've	M. they have
11. we'll	S. I am

___ ___ ___ ___ ___ ___ ___   ___ ___ ___ ___
9   4   11   6   8   1   5   7   2   10   3

4.15 Up, Down, and Around

> This man invented four-wheel roller skates in 1863. What was his name?
>   To answer the question, find the indefinite pronoun in each set of words below. Write the letter of the indefinite pronoun in the space above its line number at the bottom of the page. You will need to divide the letters into words.

1. I. anybody	U. whose	S. for	J. after
2. S. them	V. known	C. now	T. both
3. N. place	L. anyone	A. your	W. there
4. G. not	S. none	B. his	R. alone
5. E. form	C. with	O. all	L. first
6. A. any	E. its	J. once	T. upward
7. M. clever	Y. since	H. hers	N. some
8. R. then	O. thus	E. each	I. beneath
9. G. your	S. before	P. when	J. nothing
10. M. everyone	D. left	O. whomever	T. here
11. E. they	P. someone	L. soon	C. old

___ ___ ___ ___ ___ ___ ___ ___ ___ ___ ___ ___ ___
9   6   10   8   4   11   3   1   10   11   2   5   7

Name _____ Date _____

4.16 Strange Creature

This animal has no brain, no heart, no bones, and no true eyes. Water makes up about 95 percent of its body. What is it?

To answer the question, find the indefinite pronoun in each sentence below. Choose your answers from the underlined words. Write the letter of each answer in the space above its sentence number at the bottom of the page.

1. Marcia knows just about everything about the oceans.
      S   C   I   N

2. Nobody in her class knows as many facts about the sea.
     H   N   S   M

3. One of her ambitions is to be an oceanographer.
    E   A   U   R

4. There is nothing she wants to do more.
    L   Y   H   T

5. Everyone knows of her great interest in the sea.
     S   R I   B

6. She learns something new about the sea every day.
    W   F   V   M

7. Both of her parents are scientists.
    J   E   K   M

8. Each encourages Marcia to study hard.
    L   R   P   D

___ ___ ___ ___ ___ ___ ___ ___ ___
7   3   8   8   4   6   1   5   2

4.17 Stronger Than Steel

This natural material created by a common insect is stronger than steel. What is it?

To answer the question, match each pronoun on the left with its most accurate label on the right. Write the letter of each answer in the space above the pronoun's number at the bottom of the page. You will need to divide the letters into words.

1. herself	S. personal pronoun, singular, subject
2. us	S. possessive pronoun
3. who	L. personal pronoun, singular, object
4. I	I. reflexive pronoun
5. anyone	K. personal pronoun, plural, subject
6. both	R. indefinite pronoun, singular
7. him	E. personal pronoun, plural, object
8. that	D. indefinite pronoun, plural
9. yours	P. demonstrative pronoun
10. they	I. interrogative pronoun

___ ___ ___ ___ ___ ___ ___ ___ ___ ___
 9   8   3   6   2   5   4   1   7   10

4.18 Special Treat

Many people around the world consider a winkle to be a delicious delicacy. What is a winkle?

   To answer the question, complete each sentence below with the correct pronoun. Choose your answers from the words that follow each sentence. Write the letter of each answer in the space above its sentence number at the bottom of the page. You will need to divide the letters into words.

1. Roger's father, sister, and _____ go deep-sea fishing every summer.
   N. he   T. him

2. They go with some of _____ neighbors and friends.
   D. they're   B. their

3. _____ always an enjoyable trip.
   I. Its   D. It's

4. Roger always wonders _____ will catch the biggest fish.
   A. who   E. whom

5. He is looking forward to trying _____ new fishing pole.
   L. his'   I. his

6. Roger's mother packed big lunches for _____.
   L. them   B. they

7. "Make sure you have all _____ gear," said Roger's father.
   W. you're   E. your

8. _____ would be a great day.
   S. This   R. These

___ ___ ___ ___ ___ ___ ___ ___ ___ ___ ___ ___ ___ ___
 7   3   5   2   6   7   8   7   4   8   1   4   5   6

4.19 Sharp-Eyed Dog

According to animal experts, these dogs have the best eyesight of any breed of dog. What dog is this?

To answer the question, read the sentences below. Determine whether the pronouns are used correctly. If the pronoun or pronouns are used correctly, write the letter for "correct" in the space above the sentence number at the bottom of the page. If at least one pronoun in a sentence is used incorrectly, write the letter for "incorrect." You will need to reverse the letters.

1. For their birthday, Kate's parents bought she and her twin brother a puppy.
   R. Correct   O. Incorrect

2. Kate's family and her visited several dog breeders.
   I. Correct   E. Incorrect

3. Finally Kate and her brother made their choice.
   N. Correct   E. Incorrect

4. They chose a golden retriever puppy who was friendly and playful.
   D. Correct   B. Incorrect

5. As soon as Kate and her brother got home, Kate and him put an old pillow and a bowl of water in a box.
   A. Correct   U. Incorrect

6. They're mother helped them make the puppy feel safe and welcomed.
   H. Correct   R. Incorrect

7. Everyone tried to think of a good name for him.
   Y. Correct   G. Incorrect

8. "I know," said her brother. "He looks happy. That's what we should name him."
   H. Correct   L. Incorrect

9. "Its a good name for him," said Kate's mother.
   B. Correct   G. Incorrect

___   ___   ___   ___   ___   ___   ___   ___   ___
 4   3   5   1   8   7   2   6   9

Adjectives

Adjectives are words that modify nouns or pronouns. Adjectives provide details and tell *what kind*, *which one*, *how many*, or *how much*.

The tip sheets and worksheets of this section address various topics and skills related to adjectives. The first tip sheet and Worksheets 5.1 through 5.3 concentrate on identifying adjectives, while Worksheet 5.4 focuses on proper adjectives. The next tip sheet and Worksheets 5.5 through 5.7 focus on the comparison of adjectives, and Worksheets 5.8 through 5.10 provide reviews.

Adjectives

• •

Adjectives are words that describe or modify a noun or pronoun. There are different kinds of adjectives.

- Most adjectives tell *what kind, which one, how many,* or *how much.*

  The <u>icy</u> wind made me shiver. (what kind)

  The office is on the <u>third</u> floor. (which one)

  The storm dropped a <u>few</u> inches of snow. (how much)

- The words *a, an,* and *the* are special adjectives. They are called *articles. The* is a definite article. It refers to a specific person, place, thing, or idea. *A* and *an* are indefinite articles. They refer to general persons, places, things, or ideas. Use *a* before words beginning with a consonant. Use *an* before words beginning with a vowel sound.

  Have <u>the steamy soup</u> for lunch. (specific; the steamy soup)

  Have <u>a sandwich</u> for lunch. (nonspecific; any kind of sandwich)

- When used before nouns, the words *this, that, these,* and *those* are *demonstrative adjectives.* They point out specific nouns or pronouns. *This* and *these* point out nouns or pronouns that are nearby. *That* and *those* point out nouns or pronouns that are farther away. *This* and *that* come before singular nouns or pronouns. *These* and *those* come before plural nouns or pronouns.

  <u>This</u> pen is out of ink.

  <u>These</u> pencils should be used for the test.

  <u>That</u> star is bright.

  <u>Those</u> stars are faint.

  Note that when *this, that, these,* and *those* are used alone, they are called *demonstrative pronouns.*

- *Proper adjectives* are adjectives formed from proper nouns.

Proper Noun	Proper Adjective
America	American students
Greece	Greek art
China	Chinese history

• •

5.1 Time for Books

The first public library opened in this South Carolina city in 1698. What is the name of the city?

To answer the question, find the adjective in each set of words below. Write the letter of the adjective in the space above its line number at the bottom of the page.

1. K. skyscraper   E. beautiful   F. forest   W. jogged

2. O. marvelous   A. through   S. harbor   V. activity

3. Y. tropics   L. capture   C. traveler   A. dry

4. E. color   T. the   M. dinosaur   J. students

5. W. clouds   M. addition   R. fluffy   E. peak

6. N. studious   T. yesterday   A. engine   P. arrive

7. V. summit   J. package   R. sunshine   H. brilliant

8. J. answer   I. write   L. popular   O. into

9. U. offer   S. adventurous   B. fireplace   L. question

10. E. bring   I. town   C. modern   R. somebody

___ ___ ___ ___ ___ ___ ___ ___ ___ ___
10   7   3   5   8   1   9   4   2   6

Adjectives

5.2 Up and Around

In 1893, the first kind of this amusement ride was built in Chicago. What ride was this?

To answer the question, find an adjective in each sentence below. Choose your answers from among the underlined words. Write the letter beneath the adjective in the space above its sentence number at the bottom of the page. You will need to divide the letters into words.

1. Emily <u>loves</u> amusement <u>parks</u> and their <u>scariest</u> <u>rides</u>.
          D   R   I   S

2. Her <u>parents</u> buy season <u>passes</u> for the <u>entire</u> family every year.
    I   T   N   H

3. Emily <u>always</u> has a <u>fantastic</u> <u>time</u> at the park.
    O   L   H A

4. She and her <u>older</u> <u>brother</u> <u>go</u> <u>to</u> the roller-coaster first.
            W   R M T

5. Emily <u>considers</u> <u>that</u> ride to be the best <u>in</u> the <u>park</u>.
       E   S   R   M

6. Her younger <u>brother</u> is <u>afraid</u> <u>of</u> roller-<u>coasters</u>.
        N   R L   S

7. <u>The</u> <u>waterslides</u> are <u>fun</u> <u>for</u> everyone.
  E   A   I U

8. Her mother <u>and</u> father <u>enjoy</u> the <u>excellent</u> <u>shows</u>.
        G   T   F   R

___ ___ ___ ___ ___ ___ ___ ___ ___ ___ ___
 8   7   6   6   1   5   4   2   7   7   3

Adjectives

5.3 Special Soft Drink

In 1929, Charles Griggs created the soft drink that eventually came to be called 7-Up. What did Griggs originally call this drink?

To answer the question, read the article below and determine whether the underlined words are adjectives. (Not all adjectives in the article are underlined.) Starting with the first sentence, write the letters beneath the underlined adjectives in order on the blanks at the bottom of the page.

Tina <u>and</u> her <u>little</u> brother Travis planned <u>a</u> <u>big</u> surprise party <u>for</u> their mother's
     R   L   I T   C

birthday. On <u>the</u> day of the <u>party</u>, while their father <u>took</u> their mother shopping,
              H   J   S

Tina and Travis decorated the family room. They hung <u>colorful</u> streamers <u>up</u> and set
                                            I   B

the table with paper plates. Travis filled <u>plastic</u> cups <u>with</u> <u>cold</u> punch. Their grand-
                                      A   U   T

mother soon arrived with a <u>huge</u> <u>cake</u>. After <u>several</u> <u>guests</u> came, everyone waited
                               E   M   D   I

for Tina's father to bring her <u>unsuspecting</u> <u>mother</u> home. When Tina heard the car
                                    L   V

pull <u>into</u> the driveway, she <u>turned</u> out the lights. The <u>crowded</u> room was <u>silent</u>. As
     H   S   E   M

her mother <u>stepped</u> into the <u>dark</u> room, a <u>happy</u> Tina flipped on the switch.
          U   O   N

Everyone <u>yelled</u>, "Surprise!"
      D

___ ___ ___ ___ ___ ___ ___ ___ ___   ___ ___ ___ ___

Adjectives

5.4 Common Trait

About 90 percent of people throughout the world share this trait. What are these people?

To answer the question, write the missing proper noun or proper adjective below. In the parentheses after each pair, a letter is called for. Find this letter in your answer, then write the letter in the space above its number at the bottom of the page. The first one is done for you. You will need to divide the letters into words.

Proper Noun	Proper Adjective
1. Egypt	_____Egyptian_____ (fifth letter)
2. Italy	_____ (seventh letter)
3. China	_____ (fifth letter)
4. Sweden	_____ (fifth letter)
5. Mexico	_____ (sixth letter)
6. _____	_____English_____ (seventh letter)
7. Ireland	_____ (fifth letter)
8. Norway	_____ (sixth letter)
9. _____	_____Finnish_____ (seventh letter)
10. _____	_____Swiss_____ (seventh letter)
11. France	_____ (sixth letter)

__ __ __ __ T_ __ __ __ __ __ __
10   4   8 11   1   7   5   2   9   3   6

Comparison of Adjectives

Many adjectives have three forms. These are called *degrees of comparison*: the *positive*, the *comparative*, and the *superlative*. For simple description, the positive form of an adjective is used. When comparing two persons, places, things, or ideas, the comparative form is used. When comparing more than two persons, places, things, or ideas, the superlative form is used.

The green house is <u>big</u>. (positive)

The brown house is <u>bigger than the green house</u>. (comparative)

The gray house is the <u>biggest of all</u>. (superlative)

- For most one-syllable adjectives and some two-syllable adjectives, form the comparative degree by adding *-er* to the positive form. To form the superlative degree, add *-est* to the positive form. For some adjectives, a final *-e* must be dropped, a final consonant must doubled, or a final *-y* must be changed to *-i*.

Positive	Comparative	Superlative
young	younger	youngest
large	larger	largest
wet	wetter	wettest
happy	happier	happiest

- For some adjectives of two syllables and most adjectives of three or more syllables, use *more* or *most* with the positive form to show degree.

Positive	Comparative	Superlative
beautiful	more beautiful	most beautiful
thrilling	more thrilling	most thrilling

- Some adjectives have irregular forms in the comparative and superlative degrees.

Positive	Comparative	Superlative
good, well	better	best
bad, ill	worse	worst
little	less	least
many, much	more	most

© Gary Robert Muschla

5.5 Discoverer of the Circulatory System

This seventeenth-century English physician was the first person to understand the human circulatory system. Who was he?

To answer the question, write the correct form of the missing degree of comparison for each adjective. In the parentheses at the end of each set, a letter is called for. Find this letter in your answer, and write the letter in the space above the adjective's number at the bottom of the page. You will need to divide the letters into words.

Positive	Comparative	Superlative
1. good	_____	best (sixth letter)
2. grim	grimmer	_____ (fifth letter)
3. bad	_____	worst (fifth letter)
4. little	less	_____ (third letter)
5. _____	rougher	roughest (fifth letter)
6. _____	narrower	narrowest (sixth letter)
7. _____	hungrier	hungriest (sixth letter)
8. thirsty	_____	thirstiest (seventh letter)
9. _____	lovelier	loveliest (third letter)
10. wild	_____	wildest (third letter)

___ ___ ___ ___ ___ ___ ___ ___ ___ ___ ___ ___
 6   8   10   10   8   4   2   5   4   1   9   3   7

120

5.6 Slow Grower

This sea animal takes up to a hundred years to grow one-third of an inch. What is the name of this incredibly slow-growing animal?

To answer the question, complete each sentence below with the correct form of adjective. Choose your answers from the words that follow each sentence. Write the letter of each answer in the space above its sentence number at the bottom of the page. You will need to divide the letters into words.

1. The Indian Ocean is _____ than the Atlantic Ocean.
   G. small   C. smaller

2. Covering nearly sixty-four million square miles, the Pacific Ocean is the _____ ocean of all.
   N. bigger   S. biggest

3. A _____ part of the Arctic Ocean is ice-covered year-round.
   P. great   L. greatest

4. The sailfish is the _____ fish in the ocean.
   G. faster   D. fastest

5. Whales, which are mammals, are among the _____ animals on Earth.
   W. larger   L. largest

6. Many species of fish are _____ when compared to whales.
   M. tiny   R. tinier

7. Sharks have incredibly _____ jaws with sharp teeth.
   A. strong   R. stronger

8. There is no _____ sight than a sunset over the ocean.
   R. lovely   E. lovelier

___ ___ ___ ___ ___ ___ ___ ___ ___ ___ ___
 4   8   8   3   2   8   7   1   5   7   6

Adjectives

5.7 High-Protein Food

Worried that his elderly patients were not eating enough foods with protein, Dr. Ambrose Straub invented this food. What food did he invent?

To answer the question, read each sentence below. Decide whether the underlined adjective is used correctly. If the form of the adjective is correct, write the letter for "correct" in the space above its sentence number at the bottom of the page. If it is incorrect, write the letter for "incorrect." You will need to divide the letters into words.

1. Everyone should eat foods that provide a <u>more balanced</u> diet.
   S. Correct   A. Incorrect

2. Some foods contain <u>more healthy</u> ingredients than others.
   N. Correct   R. Incorrect

3. Most people should eat three <u>solid</u> meals each day.
   N. Correct   H. Incorrect

4. Most diet experts agree that skipping breakfast is a <u>biggest</u> mistake.
   A. Correct   U. Incorrect

5. Eating junk food regularly is one of the <u>baddest</u> food choices you can make.
   D. Correct   B. Incorrect

6. Few diets are <u>worse</u> than those filled with junk food.
   P. Correct   F. Incorrect

7. People need to make <u>good</u> decisions when it comes to planning their meals.
   E. Correct   I. Incorrect

8. People who are <u>more active</u> than others usually need to eat more calories each day.
   T. Correct   N. Incorrect

___ ___ ___ ___ ___ ___ ___ ___ ___ ___ ___ ___
 6   7   1   3   4   8   5   4   8   8   7   2

5.8 Galileo Galilei

Galileo Galilei was one of history's most brilliant scientists. He was one of the first men to use this device as a tool for science. What was the device?

To answer the question, match each of the underlined adjectives on the left with its most accurate label on the right. Write the letter of the label in the space above the adjective's number at the bottom of the page.

Adjective	Type of Adjective
1. <u>American</u> flag	C. definite article
2. <u>this</u> book	E. indefinite article
3. the <u>best</u> choice	T. demonstrative adjective
4. a <u>great</u> story	L. adjective, positive degree
5. <u>an</u> apple	P. adjective, comparative degree
6. <u>the</u> movie	S. adjective, superlative degree
7. <u>a</u> computer	O. proper adjective
8. the <u>better</u> one	
9. <u>a</u> house	

___ ___ ___ ___ ___ ___ ___ ___ ___
2   9   4   7   3   6   1   8   5

Adjectives

5.9 A Picture Is Worth a Thousand Words

This man invented the first handheld camera in 1888. Who was he?

To answer the question, identify the adjective in each sentence below. (Only one adjective appears in each sentence.) In the parentheses that follow each sentence, a letter is called for. Find this letter in the adjective, and write the letter in the space above the adjective's sentence number at the bottom of the page. The first one is done for you. You will need to divide the letters into words.

1. <u>Cr</u>ude photographs were made around 1831. (second letter)

2. Photography had made several advances by 1860. (first letter)

3. But primitive equipment frustrated photographers. (fourth letter)

4. By 1880 great improvements had been made in photography. (fifth letter)

5. Photographers regularly worked long hours. (second letter)

6. New equipment excited photographers. (first letter)

7. Major breakthroughs with cameras came in 1888. (second letter)

8. Significant advances improved cameras. (third letter)

9. Soon amateur photographers could be found everywhere. (fifth letter)

$$\frac{\quad}{8} \ \frac{\quad}{9} \ \frac{\quad}{5} \ \frac{R}{1} \ \frac{\quad}{8} \ \frac{\quad}{9} \ \frac{\quad}{9} \ \frac{\quad}{7} \ \frac{\quad}{2} \ \frac{\quad}{4} \ \frac{\quad}{3} \ \frac{\quad}{7} \ \frac{\quad}{6}$$

5.10 Impressive Moon

One of Jupiter's moons is the largest moon in our solar system. In fact, it is bigger than the planets Mercury and Pluto. What is the name of this moon?

To answer the question, complete each sentence below with the correct form of adjective. Choose your answers from the words that follow each sentence. Write the letter of each answer in the space above its sentence number at the bottom of the page.

1. Jupiter is the _____ planet in our solar system.
   A. most large   E. largest

2. Jupiter, the fifth planet, is _____ than Saturn, the sixth planet.
   A. more visible   U. most visible

3. Jupiter was named for the _____ god of the ancient Romans.
   S. importantest   M. most important

4. It has a(n) _____ red spot in its clouds.
   N. enormous   R. most enormous

5. This great red spot is a _____ storm.
   E. tremendous   R. most tremendous

6. This storm is thought to be the _____ in our solar system.
   R. greater   G. greatest

7. The storm is _____ than the entire Earth.
   D. bigger   E. biggest

8. Jupiter is among the _____ planets in our solar system.
   M. interestingest   Y. most interesting

___ ___ ___ ___ ___ ___ ___ ___
 6   2   4   8   3   1   7   5

Adjectives

Adverbs

When introducing adverbs to your students, explain that adverbs are words that modify verbs, adjectives, and other adverbs. They most often modify verbs and tell *how, when, where, to what extent,* or *how often* the action of the verb is done. Be sure to emphasize that many, but not all, adverbs end in *-ly*.

The tip sheets and worksheets that follow address various topics and skills related to adverbs. The first tip sheet and Worksheets 6.1 through 6.3 focus on identifying adverbs. The second tip sheet and Worksheets 6.4 through 6.6 focus on the comparison of adverbs. The third tip sheet and Worksheets 6.7 and 6.8 focus on double negatives, and Worksheets 6.9 through 6.11 offer reviews for adverbs.

Adverbs

Adverbs are words that modify verbs, adjectives, or other adverbs.

- Adverbs usually answer one of the following questions in a sentence: *How? When? Where? To what extent? How often?*

  Meg walked <u>slowly</u>. (how)

  He will arrive <u>soon</u>. (when)

  Tim stood <u>there</u>. (where)

  She <u>completely</u> believed Todd's excuse. (to what extent)

  She works out <u>daily</u>. (how often)

- Many adverbs modify verbs. An adverb that modifies a verb can appear almost anywhere in a sentence.

  <u>Finally</u>, she finished her report.

  She <u>finally</u> finished her report.

  She finished her report <u>finally</u>.

- An adverb that modifies an adjective or another adverb usually comes directly before the word it modifies.

  Grammar is an <u>extremely important</u> subject. (adverb modifying adjective)

  You must speak <u>very clearly</u> into the microphone. (adverb modifying adverb)

- Many, but not all, adverbs end in *-ly*. Following are some examples of common adverbs:

almost	always	calmly	clearly
completely	easily	entirely	extremely
here	often	politely	quite
really	recently	so	soon
suddenly	then	there	totally
very	when	where	yet

6.1 Do You Have a Middle Name?

Although they are probably familiar with Donald Duck, the famous Disney cartoon character, most people do not know Donald's middle name. What is Donald Duck's middle name?

To answer the question, find the adverb in each set of words below. Write the letter of the adverb in the space above its line number at the bottom of the page.

1. S. windy	P. happy	R. questionable	E. angrily
2. U. often	T. adventurous	A. these	I. search
3. E. library	F. interrupt	N. nearly	T. statue
4. R. dangerous	D. upon	O. soon	M. position
5. E. hurry	A. suddenly	F. description	S. darkness
6. D. advertise	C. presidential	L. eager	R. now
7. T. priceless	Y. softly	N. comfortable	W. during
8. L. extremely	F. building	O. fashionable	V. careful
9. C. panic	P. complain	F. always	D. direct
10. E. glowing	T. finally	R. unfortunate	U. occur

___ ___ ___ ___ ___ ___ ___ ___ ___ ___
 9   5   2   3   10   8   1   6   4   7

Adverbs

6.2 Just the Average Person

An average person in the United States spends about five years of his or her life doing this. What is it?

To answer the question, find the adverb in each sentence below. Choose your answers from among the underlined words. Write the letter of each answer in the space above its sentence number at the bottom of the page.

1. Recently Hannah did a report on the population of the United States.
   E   D   A   W

2. She usually finishes her reports before they are due.
   N   H   O   V

3. She is very careful in gathering information.
   M   T   Y   J

4. She researches each of her topics completely.
   R   N   T   I

5. She always finds many interesting facts.
   R   L   C   I

6. She organizes her information clearly in a detailed outline.
   S   J   A   E

7. A curious person, Hannah seldom finds her work boring.
   E   D   T   S

8. Soon Hannah will start a report on the French Revolution.
   G   N   D   S

___ ___ ___ ___ ___ ___ ___ ___
 7   5   1   6   3   4   2   8

6.3 Snakes

Able to grow up to twenty-seven feet in length, this South American snake is one of the world's biggest. What is its name?

To answer the question, read the article below and decide whether the underlined words are adverbs. Starting with the first sentence, write the letters beneath the adverbs in order on the blanks at the bottom of the page.

To <u>most</u> people, snakes are <u>extremely</u> <u>frightening</u> creatures. Although some
     P   A   R

snakes are <u>poisonous</u>, most are <u>completely</u> harmless to people. In <u>fact</u>, <u>many</u> snakes are
         Y   N   T I

<u>very</u> beneficial. They eat <u>small</u> animals and rodents, <u>effectively</u> keeping the <u>populations</u>
A   H   C   S

of <u>these</u> animals in check. But <u>this</u> <u>fact</u> is <u>seldom</u> enough to make people think <u>favorably</u>
  E   T L   O   N

of snakes. <u>Suddenly</u> <u>seeing</u> a snake slither <u>across</u> the ground is <u>often</u> a <u>startling</u>
          D   K   H   A   I

experience for <u>most</u> of us.
           N

___   ___   ___   ___   ___   ___   ___   ___

Adverbs

Comparison of Adverbs

Like adjectives, many adverbs have three forms. These are called *degrees of comparison*: the *positive*, the *comparative*, and the *superlative*.

John came early to band practice. (positive)

Lori came earlier than John. (comparative)

Joe came earliest of all. (superlative)

- To form the comparative and superlative degree for most one-syllable adverbs, add *-er* and *-est* to the positive form.

Positive	Comparative	Superlative
fast	faster	fastest
slow	slower	slowest

- To form the comparative or superlative degree for most adverbs of two or more syllables, use *more* or *most* before the positive form.

Positive	Comparative	Superlative
smoothly	more smoothly	most smoothly
recently	more recently	most recently

- Some adverbs have irregular forms in the comparative and superlative degrees.

Positive	Comparative	Superlative
well	better	best
badly	worse	worst
much	more	most
far	farther	farthest

6.4 Walking Fish

This fish, found along the tropical coasts of the Indian and Pacific oceans, can walk on land. What is the name of this unusual fish?

To answer the question, match the adverbs on the left with their correct comparative or superlative form. (Either—not both—the comparative or superlative form for each adverb is correct.) Write the letter of each answer in the space above the adverb's number at the bottom of the page.

Positive	Comparative	Superlative
1. late	I. later	E. more later
2. straight	S. straighter	U. most straightest
3. quietly	N. quietlier	E. most quietly
4. fast	L. more fast	U. fastest
5. low	D. more low	P. lowest
6. completely	K. more completely	C. much completely
7. early	R. earlier	S. most earlier
8. close	Y. more close	D. closest
9. well	F. weller	M. best
10. silently	P. more silently	K. most silentlier

__ __ __ __ __ __ __ __ __ __
9   4   8   2   6   1   10   5   3   7

Adverbs

6.5 Animal or Vegetable?

This unusual ocean-living animal appears to be a vegetable. What is its name?

To answer the question, complete each sentence below with the correct form of the adverb. Choose your answers from the words that follow each sentence. Write the letter of each answer in the space above its sentence number at the bottom of the page. You will need to divide the letters into words.

1. The oceans are home to a(n) _____ large number of unusual creatures.

   M. incredibly   R. more incredibly

2. The sailfish can swim _____ than any other fish.

   R. faster   N. fastest

3. Some sea creatures are _____ suited for living in deep water rather than shallow water.

   E. well   A. better

4. Many of these animals are among the _____ understood animals in the world.

   D. more poorly   B. most poorly

5. Fish that live near the shore are _____ studied than those that live in deep water.

   T. easily   U. more easily

6. To learn about bottom-dwelling fish, scientists dive _____ below the surface.

   S. deep   O. deeper

7. When studying sharks, divers sometimes swim _____ to them than they should.

   A. close   C. closer

8. But experienced divers _____ remain a safe distance away.

   E. usually   C. most usually

___ ___ ___ ___ ___ ___ ___ ___ ___ ___ ___
6   8   3   7   5   7   5   1   4   8   2

6.6 Super Hearing

This animal uses its incredible sense of hearing to hunt for ants, its main meal, in the darkness. What is the name of this animal?

To answer the question, read each sentence below. If the underlined adverb is used correctly, write the letter for "correct" in the space above its sentence number at the bottom of the page. If the adverb is used incorrectly, write the letter for "incorrect."

1. Recently Amanda read a book about unusual animals.
   R. Correct   D. Incorrect

2. She is particularliest interested in nocturnal animals.
   I. Correct   A. Incorrect

3. Nocturnal animals are most active latest at night.
   E. Correct   A. Incorrect

4. The senses of these animals are exceedingliest keen.
   N. Correct   R. Incorrect

5. They usually possess excellent eyesight and hearing.
   D. Correct   S. Incorrect

6. They move silently through the night in search of food.
   K. Correct   T. Incorrect

7. They are well prepared for surviving in the night than other animals.
   R. Correct   A. Incorrect

8. In order to survive, they must find food successfully in the darkness.
   V. Correct   H. Incorrect

___ ___ ___ ___ ___ ___ ___ ___
 7   3   1   5   8   2   4   6

Adverbs

Double Negatives

. . . .

A negative word is a word that means "no." Some negative words are used as adverbs. The following are common negative words: *barely, no, not (n't), hardly, nobody, nothing, neither, none, nowhere, never, no one,* and *scarcely.*

- Only one negative word is necessary to make an affirmative (positive) statement negative. Using more than one negative word in a sentence results in a double negative, which is incorrect.

    I have a cell phone. (affirmative, correct)

    I do not have a cell phone. (negative, correct)

    I do not have no cell phone. (double negative, incorrect)

- The contraction for *not* (n't) is a negative.

- To correct a double negative, substitute a positive word or drop one of the negatives.

    I don't have no money with me. (double negative)

    I don't have any money with me. (correct)

    I have no money with me. (correct)

- Remember that *barely, hardly,* and *scarcely* are negatives. Do not use them with other negative words.

    Sammi is hardly never on time. (double negative)

    Sammi is hardly ever on time. (correct)

. . . .

6.7 Move Over, Rover

In 1975, Gary Dahl sold more than a million of these objects to people. What were they?

   To answer the question, read each sentence below. Decide whether it contains a double negative. If the sentence does not contain a double negative, write the letter for "correct" in the space above the sentence number at the bottom of the page. If the sentence contains a double negative, write the letter for "incorrect." You will need to divide the letters into words.

1. Many people own a pet in the United States, but others do not.
   O. Correct   R. Incorrect

2. Tara has a dog, but she doesn't have no cat.
   N. Correct   S. Incorrect

3. Emma, Tara's cousin, can never have a dog or cat because she suffers from severe allergies.
   C. Correct   D. Incorrect

4. Emma can't barely go near animals without sneezing.
   L. Correct   T. Incorrect

5. If she didn't have no allergies, she could have a pet.
   E. Correct   K. Incorrect

6. Emma's mom suggested that Emma could have an aquarium with fish, but Emma isn't interested in fish.
   E. Correct   A. Incorrect

7. Emma might not want any fish, but she thinks she might like a parrot for a pet.
   P. Correct   S. Incorrect

8. Tara doesn't know nobody else who wants a parrot for a pet.
   A. Correct   R. Incorrect

___ ___ ___ ___ ___ ___ ___ ___
 7   6   4   8   1   3   5   2

© Gary Robert Muschla

Adverbs

6.8 Slow-Moving Animal

Most animal experts agree that this animal is the slowest-moving land mammal. It travels about six feet per minute. What is this animal?

To answer the question, complete each sentence below. Choose the correct word from the choices that follow the sentence. Write the letter of each answer in the space above its sentence number at the bottom of the page.

1. Marissa's class almost _____ go on any class trip this year.
   S. did   D. didn't

2. Because of the construction of a new middle school, there _____ no money in the school board's budget for extras like class trips.
   R. was   O. wasn't

3. Fortunately, several parents _____ willing to stand by and let that happen.
   H. were   L. weren't

4. None of these parents had _____ organized a committee before.
   H. ever   R. never

5. They started a committee that _____ stop working until it raised enough money for a class trip.
   T. would   S. wouldn't

6. I know of _____ who didn't contribute to the cause.
   C. anyone   O. no one

7. _____ objected to the committee's work.
   N. Anybody   E. Nobody

8. None of the students _____ believe it when they heard that they were going to the Museum of Natural History.
   T. could   B. couldn't

___ ___ ___ ___ ___ - ___ ___ ___ ___   ___ ___ ___ ___ ___
 8   4   2   7   7   8   6   7   1   5   3   6   8   4

Adverbs

6.9 Gazing at the Stars

When energy particles from the sun interact with the Earth's magnetic field, streams of shimmering lights appear in the sky near the North and South Poles. In the north these are commonly called the Northern Lights. What is another name for the Northern Lights?

To answer the question, identify the adverb in each sentence below. (Only one adverb appears in each sentence.) In the parentheses that follow each sentence, a letter is called for. Find this letter in the adverb, then write the letter in the space above the sentence number at the bottom of the page. The first one is done for you.

1. Jacinto has become interested in the stars <u>l</u>ately. (first letter)

2. He bought a new telescope with which he can view the stars and planets clearly. (third letter)

3. He will use his telescope soon. (first letter)

4. He has wanted a new telescope for a terribly long time. (sixth letter)

5. Jacinto is particularly impressed with its powerful magnification. (seventh letter)

6. He quickly focuses on the moon. (third letter)

7. He will use his new telescope often. (first letter)

8. He eagerly shifts his telescope from the moon to a star. (fifth letter)

9. Jacinto greatly enjoys studying space. (fourth letter)

$$\underline{}\ \underline{}\ \underline{}\ \underline{}\ \underline{}\ \underline{} \qquad \underline{}\ \underline{}\ \underline{}\ \underline{}\ \underline{}\ \underline{L}\ \underline{}\ \underline{}$$
$$9 \quad 5 \quad 8 \quad 7 \quad 8 \quad 9 \qquad\quad 4 \quad 7 \quad 8 \quad 2 \quad 9 \quad 1 \quad 6 \quad 3$$

Adverbs

6.10 Revolutionary General

The nickname of this general of the American Revolution was the Swamp Fox. What was this general's real name?

To answer the question, find the comparative or superlative form of each adverb below. After writing the correct form, find the letter called for in your answer. Write this letter in the space above the adverb's number at the bottom of the page. The first one is done for you.

1. completely   Superlative: most **c**ompletely (fifth letter)

2. well   Superlative: _____ (third letter)

3. silently   Comparative: _____ (ninth letter)

4. safely   Superlative: _____ (sixth letter)

5. keenly   Comparative: _____ (first letter)

6. badly   Superlative: _____ (second letter)

7. much   Comparative: _____ (third letter)

8. often   Comparative: _____ (sixth letter)

9. early   Superlative: _____ (fifth letter)

__ __ __ __ C __ __   __ __ __ __ __ __
 8   7   4   3 1 9   2   5   4   7   9   6   3

Adverbs

© Gary Robert Muschla

140

6.11 Biggest Deer in America

This animal belongs to the deer family. Although it is the biggest deer in America, most people do not think of it as being a deer. What is the common name of this animal?

To answer the question, complete each sentence below with the correct adverb. Choose your answers from the words that follow each sentence. Write the letter of each answer in the space above its sentence number at the bottom of the page. You will need to divide the letters into words.

1. About forty species of deer are found _____ throughout the world.
   N. widely   D. most widely

2. Deer live _____ in forests and on open land.
   N. muchly   E. mostly

3. In the past, the deer population in our state was _____ declining.
   I. slow   L. slowly

4. In our area, deer have become _____ numerous in recent years.
   O. much   K. more

5. In some parts of our state, people must drive _____ to avoid colliding with deer on the roads.
   E. careful   S. carefully

6. While driving home the other night, Jill came _____ to hitting a deer.
   M. close   E. closer

7. Although she avoided an accident, she was _____ shaken up.
   O. terribly   L. more terribly

8. The problem of the increasing population of deer has become _____ than anyone expected.
   A. worse   B. worst

___ ___ ___ ___ ___ ___ ___ ___ ___ ___ ___ ___
 8   3   8   5   4   8   1   6   7   7   5   2

Adverbs

Prepositions, Conjunctions, and Interjections

The final three parts of speech are prepositions, conjunctions, and interjections. Explain to your students that, like the other parts of speech, each has a specific function in a sentence.

A *preposition* relates a noun or pronoun to another word in a sentence. All of the words related by a preposition, as well as the preposition itself, are a part of a prepositional phrase. The first two tip sheets and Worksheets 7.1 through 7.7 focus on prepositions and prepositional phrases.

A *conjunction* is a word that joins words or groups of words in a sentence. Several kinds of conjunctions, including *coordinating* conjunctions, *correlative* conjunctions, and *subordinating* conjunctions are covered in the following pages. The third tip sheet and Worksheets 7.8 and 7.9 focus on the various types of conjunctions.

An *interjection* is a word that shows feeling or emotion. The fourth tip sheet and Worksheet 7.10 focus on interjections.

This section concludes with Worksheets 7.11 through 7.14, which review the parts of speech.

Prepositions and Prepositional Phrases

A *preposition* is a word that relates a noun or pronoun to another word in a sentence. Following are examples of common prepositions.

about	before	by	near	to
above	behind	during	of	toward
across	below	for	off	under
after	beneath	from	on	underneath
along	beside	in	out	with
around	between	inside	over	within
at	beyond	into	through	without

- The noun or pronoun that follows a preposition is called the *object of the preposition.*

- A preposition, its object, and any words that modify the object are called a *prepositional phrase.*

  We went <u>into the house.</u> (The preposition is *into*, *house* is its object, and *the* is an article modifying *house.*)

- Some prepositions are made up of two or more words.

  They walked <u>out of</u> the back door.

- A preposition may have a compound object (two or more).

  He started working <u>with paint and brush.</u>

  The package was addressed <u>to John and his brother.</u>

7.1 Lady's First

On June 16, 1963, Valentina Tereshkova became the first woman to accomplish this feat. What did she do?

To answer the question, find the preposition in each set of words below. Write the letter of the preposition in the space above its line number at the bottom of the page. You will need to divide the letters into words.

1. C. the   R. yard   L. along   N. my

2. W. too   N. over   E. is   O. your

3. V. during   M. are   S. had   H. an

4. K. we   P. for   A. any   U. those

5. R. front   G. some   W. more   C. after

6. I. without   M. can   E. three   A. decide

7. I. tell   J. us   R. in   O. word

8. S. at   B. real   T. does   I. and

9. R. four   N. or   F. else   T. between

10. O. sad   R. be   A. from   M. a

11. N. see   E. across   U. not   S. jump

___ ___ ___ ___ ___ ___ ___ ___ ___ ___ ___ ___ ___
 9   7   10 3   11 1   6   2   8   4   10 5   11

7.2 Super Winds

Moving at speeds sometimes beyond 250 miles per hour, this powerful wind is found high in the atmosphere. What is this wind called?

To answer the question, read the article below. Determine whether the underlined words are prepositions. Starting with the first sentence, write the letters beneath the prepositions in order on the blanks at the bottom of the page. You will need to reverse and divide the letters into words.

Megan has <u>always</u> been interested <u>in</u> the weather. One <u>of</u> her goals is to become <u>a</u>
　　　　　　　　　S　　　　　　　　　　　　　　M　　　　　　　A　　　　　　　　　　　　　　　F

meteorologist someday. She is fascinated <u>with</u> storms <u>and</u> the movement <u>of</u> weather
　　　　　　　　　　　　　　　　　　　　　　E　　　　　　U　　　　　　　　　　　R

systems. She is <u>also</u> concerned <u>about</u> global warming. She thinks global warming will
　　　　　　　　　A　　　　　　　　T

one day change the climate <u>all</u> <u>over</u> the Earth. Megan is a <u>keen</u> observer <u>of</u> the weather.
M　　　　　　　　　　　　　　　H　S　　　　　　　　　　　　L　　　　　　　T

She studies weather maps and predicts <u>what</u> the weather will <u>be</u> <u>for</u> her town. Some <u>of</u>
　　　　　　　　　　　　　　　　　　　I　　　　　　　　　　U　E　　　　　　　J

her predictions are <u>very</u> accurate.
　　　　　　　　S

__ 　 __ 　 __ 　 __ 　 __ 　 __ 　 __ 　 __ 　 __ 　 __

Name _____ Date _____

7.3 Brain Power

The human brain is a remarkable organ made up of nerve cells. According to scientists, about how many nerve cells make up the average human brain?

To answer the question, read each sentence below and identify the prepositional phrase. In the parentheses that follow, a letter is called for. Find this letter in the prepositional phrase. Write the letter in the space above the phrase's sentence number at the bottom of the page. The first one is done for you. You will need to divide the letters into words.

1. The human brain is divided <u>into three parts</u>: the cerebrum, the cerebellum, and the medulla. (seventh letter)

2. The brain is often compared to a computer. (eighth letter)

3. The functions of the brain are exceedingly complex. (sixth letter)

4. Your brain is always active, even during sleep. (first letter)

5. The largest part of this organ is the cerebrum. (fifth letter)

6. Thinking takes place in the cerebrum. (second letter)

7. The cerebellum controls movement of the body. (fourth letter)

8. Your heart, breathing, and other involuntary systems are controlled by the medulla. (seventh letter)

9. Scientists will be studying the human brain for a long time. (fifth letter)

10. In the coming years they will surely learn more. (seventh letter)

___ ___ ___ ___ ___ ___ ___ R̲ ___ ___ ___ ___ ___ ___ ___ ___ ___
10 6   8   7   2   6   4   1   8   4   3   5   9   9   5 10   6

Prepositions, Conjunctions, and Interjections

© Gary Robert Muschla

147

7.4 Long-Tailed Mammal

The tail of this small mammal is almost twice as long as its body. This animal is related to the raccoon and lives in tropical regions of the Western Hemisphere. What is it?

To answer the question, read each sentence below. Find the object of the preposition in each prepositional phrase. Choose your answers from the words that follow the sentence. Write the letter of each answer in the space above its sentence number at the bottom of the page.

1. Countless animals live in the world's tropical regions.
   U. world's   A. regions

2. Many of these animals are unusual and seldom seen.
   N. animals   R. seldom

3. They remain hidden in remote areas.
   E. remote   O. areas

4. Dense rain forests provide food and shelter for these creatures.
   S. rain forests   K. creatures

5. Scientists believe that many species have not yet been discovered in tropical forests.
   O. species   I. forests

6. In time scientists will likely discover many more animals.
   J. time   W. animals

7. Our world is a wondrous planet teeming with life.
   L. planet   K. life

8. The great diversity of creatures is truly astonishing.
   U. creatures   S. astonishing

__ __ __ __ __ __ __ __
7   5   2   4   1   6   3   8

Prepositional Phrases as Adjectives and Adverbs

Prepositional phrases can modify nouns, pronouns, verbs, adjectives, and adverbs.

- When a prepositional phrase modifies a noun or pronoun, it is called an *adjective phrase.* Like adjectives, adjectives phrases answer the questions *What kind? Which one? How much?* and *How many?* Adjective phrases usually follow the noun or pronoun they modify.

  This is a book of ancient art. (The prepositional phrase modifies the noun *book.*)

  A girl with blonde hair claimed the book. (The prepositional phrase modifies *girl.*)

- When a prepositional phrase modifies a verb, adjective, or an adverb, it is called an *adverb phrase.* Adverb phrases answer the questions *How? When? Where? How often?* and *To what extent?*

  They left in the evening. (The prepositional phrase modifies the verb *left.*)

  Val is happy with her report card. (The prepositional phrase modifies the adjective *happy.*)

  Jim reads late at night. (The prepositional phrase modifies the adverb *late.*)

7.5 Measuring the Earth's Circumference

Over two thousand years ago, this Greek mathematician, astronomer, and geographer estimated the circumference of the Earth with surprising accuracy. By some accounts, he was off by only a few hundred miles. What was his name?

To answer the question, find the adjective phrase in each sentence below. Write the letter beneath each underlined adjective phrase in the space above its sentence number at the bottom of the page.

1. The civilization of ancient Greece flourished nearly 2,500 years ago.
                          N   R

2. Long ago Greek thinkers studied the mysteries of the world.
      I   A

3. They tirelessly sought knowledge about life.
        E   R

4. Many discoveries of the ancient Greeks were truly remarkable.
                    H   T

5. Theirs was a brilliant age of exceptional achievement.
              U   O

6. They invented myths about things they could not hope to understand.
                        T   S

7. We still tell these stories of heroes and gods.
          N   S

8. Our modern society owes a great deal to the ancient Greeks.
                          A   E

___ ___ ___ ___ ___ ___ ___ ___ ___ ___ ___ ___
 8   3   2   6   5   7   6   4   8   1   8   7

7.6 Unique Weather Phenomenon

These weather phenomena occur almost nowhere else other than in North America, especially the United States. What are they?

To answer the question, find the adverb phrase in each sentence below. Write the letter beneath each underlined adverb phrase in the space above its sentence number at the bottom of the page. You will need to reverse the letters.

1. Many different kinds of weather are found throughout the United States.
   E   A

2. Damage of incredible scale can result from some storms.
   I   R

3. Massive storms with frightening power can spread across several states.
   O   E

4. Tasha's family lives near the coast, where hurricanes are a danger.
   N   S

5. When a hurricane threatens, they prepare for the storm.
   M   S

6. If necessary, the family will go to a safe place.
   A   O

7. They can stay with Tasha's grandmother, who lives a hundred miles from the coast.
   T   H

8. Great storms almost always come with heavy precipitation and powerful winds.
   R   D

__ __ __ __ __ __ __ __ __
5   3   6   8   1   4   2   6   7

7.7 Watch Out for High Tide

Rising about seventy feet, the highest tide in the world occurs in south-eastern Canada. Where exactly does this tide occur?

To answer the question, find an adjective or adverb phrase in the sentences below. In the parentheses after each sentence, a specific phrase and a letter are called for. Find the letter in the phrase, then write the letter in the space above its sentence number at the bottom of the page. The first one is done for you. You will need to divide the letters into words.

1. The tides around the world are caused <u>by the moo**n**</u>. (adverb phrase, ninth letter)

2. The waters of the oceans are affected by the moon's gravity. (adjective phrase, sixth letter)

3. The changes of the tides vary around the world. (adverb phrase, sixth letter)

4. The difference between high and low tide is great in some places. (adjective phrase, first letter)

5. The boats of careless sailors can be stranded during low tide. (adverb phrase, second letter)

6. People of ancient times were puzzled by the falling and rising water. (adverb phrase, sixth letter)

7. Captains of old sailing vessels would leave with the outgoing tide. (adjective phrase, seventh letter)

8. Ships of today still sail with the tide whenever possible. (adjective phrase, seventh letter)

$$\underset{4}{\rule{1cm}{0.4pt}} \quad \underset{7}{\rule{1cm}{0.4pt}} \quad \underset{8}{\rule{1cm}{0.4pt}} \quad \underset{2}{\rule{1cm}{0.4pt}} \quad \underset{6}{\rule{1cm}{0.4pt}} \quad \underset{6}{\rule{1cm}{0.4pt}} \quad \underset{5}{\rule{1cm}{0.4pt}} \quad \underset{1}{\overset{N}{\rule{1cm}{0.4pt}}} \quad \underset{3}{\rule{1cm}{0.4pt}} \quad \underset{8}{\rule{1cm}{0.4pt}}$$

Conjunctions

· ·

Conjunctions are words that connect words or groups of words in a sentence.

- *Coordinating* conjunctions include the words *and, but, or,* or *nor.* They connect words, phrases, and sentences.

  Monica <u>and</u> Lena are best friends.

  They went to the mall <u>and</u> to the movies.

  I thought it would snow, <u>but</u> it rained instead.

  Louis will play third base, <u>or</u> he will pitch in tonight's game.

- Correlative conjunctions are pairs of words. The following are examples of correlative conjunctions:

  either . . . or   neither . . . nor   not only . . . but also   both . . . and

  Loaded with homework, I had <u>neither</u> the time <u>nor</u> the energy to play video games.

  Tara is <u>not only</u> president of the student council <u>but also</u> secretary of the Spanish club.

- *Subordinating* conjunctions are words that begin adverb clauses. The following are examples of subordinating conjunctions:

after	as long as	if	though	whenever
although	as soon as	since	unless	where
as	because	so that	until	wherever
as if	before	then	when	while

  <u>As soon as</u> the shower ends, we will finish the game.

  <u>While</u> waiting for her brother, Danielle read her novel.

  Ming didn't know <u>where</u> he had left his keys.

· ·

Prepositions, Conjunctions, and Interjections

7.8 A Lot of Snow

One of the highest yearly snowfall totals ever recorded occurred in Washington state in the winter of 1971–1972. Over 1,224 inches (about 102 feet!) of snow fell. At what place did this occur?

To answer the question, find the coordinating or subordinating conjunction in each set of words below. Write the letter of the conjunction in the space above its line number at the bottom of the page. You will need to divide the letters into words.

1. S. on	A. and	P. over	E. your
2. A. with	W. front	O. as	T. forward
3. D. the	M. its	U. seldom	E. wherever
4. L. low	R. left	K. was	I. or
5. T. while	C. more	U. one	R. an
6. N. on	U. but	I. first	W. quite
7. V. backward	J. move	R. because	P. had
8. S. is	M. four	O. each	N. unless
9. M. although	S. soon	K. real	B. were
10. R. when	H. there	V. none	J. by
11. E. new	I. slowly	N. since	A. these
12. S. off	U. at	T. end	I. if

__ __ __ __ __ __ __ __ __ __ __ __
 9   2   6   8   5   10   1   4   11   12   3   7

7.9 Poison Ivy

Despite its name, poison ivy is not poisonous. But it does contain a substance that causes allergic reactions in many people. What is the name of this substance?

To answer the question, find the coordinating or subordinating conjunction in each sentence below. Choose your answers from among the underlined words. Write the letter of each answer in the space above its sentence number at the bottom of the page.

1. Rebecca is extremely allergic to poison ivy and poison sumac.
  U   C   A   S

2. If she touches a leaf of one of these plants, she suffers a reaction.
  I   K E   R

3. Her brother is not allergic to these plants, but her sister is.
              W   I H   R

4. Whenever Rebecca is outside, she tries to avoid these plants.
  U   N   J   T

5. She has been allergic to poison ivy since she was four years old.
         C   H   R O

6. Poison ivy may be in her backyard, or it might be nearby.
           M   W   U   E

7. Although she is careful, she suffers from it every summer.
  L   U   S   J

8. Rebecca uses a soothing cream until the reaction ends.
         C   E   O   D

___ ___ ___ ___ ___ ___ ___ ___
 6   3   4   1   5   2   8   7

Interjections

An *interjection* is a word or group of words that expresses feeling or emotion. Interjections have no grammatical relationship to any other word in a sentence. The following list contains common interjections.

aha	hooray	oh	phew
good grief	my goodness	oh, dear	well
great	gee	oh, no	wow
hey	ouch	oops	ugh

- An interjection that expresses a strong feeling is followed by an exclamation point. Such interjections stand alone, either before or after a sentence.

  Oh, no! I left my book report at home.

  Ouch! I stubbed my toe.

  I got an A on my project. Wow!

- An interjection that expresses a milder feeling usually appears at the beginning of a sentence and is followed by a comma.

  Oh, I forgot to call Jimmy.

  Gee, I'm not sure about that.

7.10 Spinning Round and Round

North of the equator, hurricanes, cyclones, and typhoons spin in a counter-clockwise direction. South of the equator, storms spin in the opposite direction. Why is this so?

To answer the question, find the interjection in each sentence below. In the parentheses after each sentence, a letter is called for. Find this letter in the interjection, and write the letter in the space above its sentence number at the bottom of the page. The first one is done for you. You will need to divide the letters into words.

1. I haven't started my report about the Earth for science. Good grie**f**! (ninth letter)

2. Yikes! I also have a book report due on the same day. (second letter)

3. Oh, no! I just remembered I have a history assignment, too. (third letter)

4. Hey, things could be worse. (second letter)

5. At least I have no other assignments. Phew! (second letter)

6. Oops, I forgot about math. (first letter)

7. That is one more thing to do. Great! (fifth letter)

8. Ah, if I start right now, I'll be able to finish everything. (first letter)

9. Hooray! I'm done. (fourth letter)

```
 __   __   __   __   __   __   __   __   __   _F_   __   __   __   __   __
  9    6    7    8    7    2    6    3    6    1     4    8    9    7    5
```

7.11 Unusual Bird

Although this bird cannot fly, it is an excellent swimmer. What is it?

To answer the question, read each sentence below. Determine whether all of the underlined words make up prepositional phrases. If all of the underlined words are prepositional phrases, write the letter for "correct" in the space above the sentence number at the bottom of the page. If any underlined words in the sentence are not a part of a prepositional phrase, or if a prepositional phrase is not entirely underlined, write the letter for "incorrect." You will need to divide the letters into words.

1. Annie enjoys going to wilderness areas with her mother.
   U. Correct   A. Incorrect

2. While in these places, they observe birds and other wildlife.
   D. Correct   E. Incorrect

3. Annie's mother is a biologist who studies animals in their natural environment.
   R. Correct   A. Incorrect

4. Annie would like to be a biologist someday and help her mother with her work.
   S. Correct   N. Incorrect

5. While working together, they have observed many interesting animals in many surroundings.
   E. Correct   P. Incorrect

6. Although her mother is most interested in mammals, Annie is more interested in birds.
   I. Correct   K. Incorrect

7. Along with eagles, Annie is especially interested in hawks and falcons.
   N. Correct   H. Incorrect

8. In Annie's opinion, being a biologist is the best job in the world.
   G. Correct   A. Incorrect

___ ___ ___ ___ ___ ___ ___ ___
 3   5   2   7   8   1   6   4

7.12 Fresh Water

Nearly 20 percent of the world's fresh water is found in these bodies of water. What are they called?

To answer the question, read each sentence below. Determine whether the underlined prepositional phrase is used as an adjective or adverb. If the phrase is used as an adjective, write the letter for "adjective" in the space above its sentence number at the bottom of the page. If the phrase is used as an adverb, write the letter for "adverb." You will need to reverse and divide the letters into words.

1. About 70 percent of the Earth is covered <u>with water</u>.
   Z. Adjective   T. Adverb

2. Most of the world's water is contained <u>in the oceans</u>.
   R. Adjective   L. Adverb

3. Water is essential <u>for life</u>.
   M. Adjective   R. Adverb

4. Many different kinds <u>of animals</u> require fresh water to survive.
   S. Adjective   N. Adverb

5. Fresh water is found <u>in ponds, rivers, and lakes</u>.
   A. Adjective   E. Adverb

6. Great amounts <u>of fresh water</u> are trapped in ice at the Earth's poles.
   K. Adjective   L. Adverb

7. If the ice <u>at the poles</u> melted, sea levels would rise hundreds of feet.
   G. Adjective   A. Adverb

8. Some <u>of the world's biggest cities</u> would be flooded.
   A. Adjective   O. Adverb

___   ___   ___   ___   ___   ___   ___   ___   ___   ___
4   5   6   8   2   1   8   5   3   7

Name _____   Date _____

7.13 Very Old Fish

Scientists consider the paddlefish to be a living fossil. It has been around for about 230 million years. It is found in two places today. One of these places is China. What is the other?

To answer the question, match the words and phrases that follow with their most accurate label. Choose your answers from the terms below the words. Write the letter of each answer in the space above its number at the bottom of the page. If there is no match, write the letter for "no match." You will need to divide the letters into words.

1. while   2. of   3. although   4. to

5. during school   6. as soon as   7. and   8. unless

9. because   10. oh, no   11. for   12. at

13. but   14. in the garden 15. evening   16. either . . . or

Answers

S. Preposition
R. Coordinating conjunction
I. Subordinating conjunction
E. Interjection
V. Correlative conjunction
P. Prepositional phrase
M. No match

15   6   2   11   9   4   12   1   14   5   8   13   3   16   10   7

7.14 Making Waves

An earthquake is a shaking of the Earth's crust. When an earthquake occurs beneath the sea, powerful waves may result. What is the Japanese name for these great waves?

To answer the question, name the part of speech of the underlined word in each sentence below. Choose your answers from the parts of speech that follow the sentences. Write the letter of each answer in the space above its sentence number at the bottom of the page. One answer is not used.

1. Wind causes most waves <u>on</u> the ocean.

2. When winds blow <u>lightly</u>, waves are small and gentle.

3. <u>Powerful</u> winds can cause great storms and waves.

4. Victoria <u>lives</u> on the East Coast, close to the sea.

5. She enjoys swimming <u>and</u> surfing.

6. She and <u>her</u> friends love the beach.

7. Victoria is always sad when the <u>summer</u> ends.

Answers

M. noun
I. verb
T. adjective
S. conjunction
A. pronoun
U. adverb
O. interjection
N. preposition

___ ___ ___ ___ ___ ___ ___
3   5   2   1   6   7   4

Punctuation and Capitalization

A sound understanding of punctuation and capitalization is essential to understanding grammar. Punctuation and capitalization help to make written expression clear. Suggest to your students that they imagine a paragraph composed of sentences with no punctuation marks or capital letters. Such a paragraph would no doubt be a challenge to read.

The tip sheets and worksheets that follow concentrate on punctuation and capitalization. The first tip sheet and Worksheets 8.1 and 8.2 address abbreviations. The tip sheets and worksheets from 8.3 through 8.18 focus on specific punctuation—end marks, commas, colons, semicolons, apostrophes, quotation marks, and italics—while Worksheets 8.19 through 8.28 offer general reviews of punctuation. The final tip sheet and Worksheets 8.29 through 8.33 focus on capitalization, with Worksheet 8.34 providing a review of capitalization.

Abbreviations

Abbreviations are shortened forms of words. Many abbreviations start with a capital letter and end with a period. A list of common abbreviations follows.

Days of the Week

Sun.	Sunday
Mon.	Monday
Tues.	Tuesday
Wed.	Wednesday
Thurs.	Thursday
Fri.	Friday
Sat.	Saturday

Months

Jan.	January
Feb.	February
Mar.	March
Apr.	April
Jun.	June
Jul.	July
Aug.	August
Sept.	September
Oct.	October
Nov.	November
Dec.	December

Streets

St.	Street
Rd.	Road
Ave.	Avenue
Blvd.	Boulevard
Dr.	Drive

Titles

Mr.	Mister
Mrs.	Mistress

Titles (continued)

Pres.	President
Dr.	Doctor
Capt.	Captain
Lt.	Lieutenant
Hon.	Honorable
Gov.	Governor
Sr.	Senior
Jr.	Junior

The abbreviations for some companies, government agencies, and institutions use capital letters and no periods. Here are some examples:

ABC	American Broadcasting Company
CBS	Columbia Broadcasting System
CIA	Central Intelligence Agency
EPA	Environmental Protection Agency
FBI	Federal Bureau of Investigation
IRS	Internal Revenue Service
MIT	Massachusetts Institute of Technology
NBC	National Broadcasting Company
PBS	Public Broadcasting System
USA	United States of America

8.1 High-Speed Diver

This bird can dive after prey at speeds up to 175 miles per hour. What is the name of this bird?

To answer the question, match each word with its abbreviation. Write the letter of each answer in the space above its number at the bottom of the page. You will need to divide the letters into words.

1. Boulevard	E. Bld.	A. Blvd.
2. August	I. Aug.	U. Augt.
3. Tuesday	L. Ts.	R. Tues.
4. President	E. Pre.	R. Pres.
5. November	R. Nor.	N. Nov.
6. Doctor	L. Dr.	S. D.
7. Drive	O. Dr.	M. De.
8. Street	G. St.	D. S.
9. Governor	F. Gov.	C. Gr.
10. April	R. Ap.	C. Apr.
11. Junior	S. J.	P. Jr.
12. Captain	E. Capt.	A. Cap.

___ ___ ___ ___ ___ ___ ___ ___ ___ ___ ___ ___ ___ ___
11 12 3 12 8 4 2 5 12 9 1 6 10 7 5

Punctuation and Capitalization

8.2 Inventor of the Popsicle

In 1905, this eleven-year-old boy was mixing powdered soda and water to make soda pop. He accidentally left the mixture outside overnight, and it froze. The next morning he discovered what would come to be called *popsicles*. What was this boy's name?

To answer the question, write the full word that makes up each abbreviation. In the parentheses after each term, a letter is called for. Find this letter in your answer, then write it in the space above its number at the bottom of the page. The first one is done for you. You will need to divide the letters into words.

1. Pl.   _____**P**lace_____ (first letter)

2. Ave.   _____ (sixth letter)

3. Capt.   _____ (seventh letter)

4. Wed.   _____ (fifth letter)

5. Nov.   _____ (eighth letter)

6. Sat.   _____ (fifth letter)

7. Gov.   _____ (sixth letter)

8. Sept.   _____ (third letter)

9. Pkwy.   _____ (fourth letter)

10. Oct.   _____ (fourth letter)

11. Feb.   _____ (first letter)

12. Blvd.   _____ (seventh letter)

13. Thur.   _____ (fifth letter)

```
 __   __   __   __   __   __   __    P   __   __   __   __   __
 11   5    12   3    9    4    8     1    2    6    13   10   7
```

End Punctuation and Periods

· ·

End punctuation includes periods, question marks, and exclamation points. Because they end sentences and indicate the end of abbreviations and initials, these are some of the most important marks of punctuation.

- A period ends a statement or command.

  It looks like rain.

  We will go shopping on Saturday.

  Please close the door.

- A question mark ends a question.

  Will it rain tonight?

  Do you think we'll have homework for the weekend?

  What page are the math problems on?

- An exclamation point ends an exclamation.

  Watch out!

  Oh, no! I forgot to do my homework.

  What a catch! Wow!

- Use a period in most abbreviations and after initials.

Mr.	Mrs.
Dr.	Capt.
Ave.	St.
J. K. Rowling	John F. Kennedy

8.3 Long-Distance Flyers

These birds have the longest migration of any birds, over twenty thousand miles each year. What is the name of these birds?

To answer the question, read each sentence below. If the end punctuation is correct, write the letter for "correct" in the space above the sentence number at the bottom of the page. If the end punctuation is incorrect, write the letter for "incorrect." You will need to divide the letters into words.

1. Many species of birds migrate long distances.
   I. Correct   E. Incorrect

2. Some species fly thousands of miles each year.
   E. Correct   A. Incorrect

3. Do you know of any of these species!
   N. Correct   S. Incorrect

4. Please look up the migration routes for birds?
   B. Correct   A. Incorrect

5. Where is the best place to find that information.
   E. Correct   N. Incorrect

6. I wonder which bird has the longest migration route?
   A. Correct   C. Incorrect

7. Not all birds migrate.
   R. Correct   A. Incorrect

8. Migrations usually coincide with the seasons.
   T. Correct   M. Incorrect

___ ___ ___ ___ ___ ___ ___ ___ ___ ___ ___
 4   7   6   8   1   6   8   2   7   5   3

Punctuation and Capitalization

Commas

· ·

Commas have a variety of uses in sentences. Use a comma for the following:

- To separate the words in a series.

    They packed sandwiches, fruits, and snacks in the picnic basket.

- Before the coordinate conjunctions *and*, *but*, *or*, or *nor* when forming a compound sentence.

    Tina wanted to go to the movies, but Rachel wanted to go to the mall.

- To set off introductory words, phrases, and clauses.

    No, it hasn't started snowing yet.

    Pleased with her report card, Marcy smiled broadly.

    If he finished his homework early, Bradley would have time to play a video game.

- To set off appositives and parenthetical expressions.

    Kimberly, John's younger sister, was always causing mischief.

    In my opinion, students do not receive enough homework.

    Most students, of course, believe they receive too much homework.

- Between the name of a city or town and state.

    Boston, Massachusetts

    Jackson, New Jersey

    Port Richey, Florida

- Between the day and year in a date.

    June 1, 2008

    August 21, 2008

- After the greeting in a friendly letter, and after the closing in all letters.

    Dear Uncle Jim,

    Sincerely,

    Yours truly,

(continued)

· ·

Commas (continued)

- To set off nouns in direct address.

  Jason, it's time to go.

  I told you, Lori, we have to go to the store first.

- To set off direct quotations in a sentence.

  "The basketball game starts at seven," said Ben.

  Jenna said, "I hope we're not late for the game."

  "After I finish my homework," said Brad, "I'll watch the game."

- To separate adjectives of equal importance.

  The tall, blonde woman walking toward them had to be Natalia's aunt.

- In numbers of more than three digits.

  1,999

  20,478

  108,423

8.4 Visiting Paris

This landmark in Paris is a prime attraction for tourists. What is its name?

To answer the question, read each sentence below. If the commas in the sentence are used correctly, write the letter for "correct" in the space above the sentence number at the bottom of the page. If at least one comma in the sentence is missing or is used incorrectly, write the letter for "incorrect." You will need to reverse and divide the letters into words.

1. Melissa, and her family went to Europe last summer, and they visited London, Paris, and Rome.
   R. Correct   O. Incorrect

2. Melissa found these cities to be wonderful, but her little sister Megan would have preferred to go to the beach instead.
   I. Correct   H. Incorrect

3. Jonathan, Melissa's brother thought that Paris was the most interesting city.
   E. Correct   W. Incorrect

4. Melissa, on the other hand, felt that Rome was more interesting.
   R. Correct   L. Incorrect

5. While in Rome the family, visited Melissa's great-grandmother.
   O. Correct   T. Incorrect

6. Of course, it was exciting to visit all of the countries.
   L. Correct   E. Incorrect

7. A trip to Europe, in my opinion would be a great experience.
   T. Correct   F. Incorrect

8. As she packed to return home, Melissa already looked forward to visiting Europe again.
   E. Correct   T. Incorrect

___ ___ ___ ___ ___ ___ ___ ___ ___ ___ ___
 4   8   3   1   5   6   8   7   7   2   8

8.5 Continental City

This is the only city in the world that is located on two continents. What is its name?

To answer the question, read each sentence below. If the end punctuation and commas are used correctly, write the letter for "correct" in the space above the sentence number at the bottom of the page. If the end punctuation or a comma is missing, or is used incorrectly, write the letter for "incorrect."

1. A continent is a large land mass.
   T. Correct   M. Incorrect

2. Most geographers divide the Earth into seven continents, but some, consider Europe and Asia to be parts of one huge continent.
   E. Correct   N. Incorrect

3. This huge continent is usually referred to as Eurasia.
   S. Correct   O. Incorrect

4. Europe and Asia, in my opinion, are separate continents.
   U. Correct   E. Incorrect

5. What is your opinion on that.
   R. Correct   A. Incorrect

6. I wonder what percentage of geographers consider Europe and Asia to be a single continent?
   M. Correct   I. Incorrect

7. Of all the continents, Asia, has the largest population.
   S. Correct   L. Incorrect

8. The continent with the smallest human population, of course, is Antarctica.
   B. Correct   M. Incorrect

___ ___ ___ ___ ___ ___ ___ ___
 6   3   1   5   2   8   4   7

8.6 Biggest Island

This is the biggest island in the world. What is its name?

To answer the question, read each sentence below. Determine whether the end marks and commas are used correctly. If an end mark is missing or is used incorrectly, write the letter for "end mark" in the space above the sentence number at the bottom of the page. If a comma is missing or is used incorrectly, write the letter for "comma." If the sentence is correct, write the letter for "no mistake." You will need to reverse the letters.

1. Islands are small, bodies of land surrounded by water.
   S. End mark   A. Comma   E. No mistake

2. The only difference between an island, and a continent is size.
   U. End mark   N. Comma   A. No mistake

3. Having an area of about 2.9 million square miles, Australia is the smallest continent
   D. End mark   L. Comma   R. No mistake

4. No island, therefore, can be larger than Australia.
   H. End mark   W. Comma   N. No mistake

5. Great Britain is an island country that is located off the western coast of France.
   U. End mark   A. Comma   R. No mistake

6. Some islands, such as the Hawaiian Islands were formed by volcanoes.
   T. End mark   L. Comma   N. No mistake

7. Many islands are home to countless plants, animals, and people.
   N. End mark   S. Comma   E. No mistake

8. I'd like to know how many people live on islands throughout the world?
   G. End mark   B. Comma   I. No mistake

___ ___ ___ ___ ___ ___ ___ ___ ___
 3   4   1   6   2   7   7   5   8

Colons and Semicolons

Colons and semicolons have special uses. Use a colon for the following:

- To set off words in a list.

  Louisa wrote down the items she needed for the party: napkins, paper plates, paper cups, and decorations.

- Between hours and minutes in time.

  9:30 A.M.

  7:45 P.M.

- After the greeting of a business letter.

  Dear Ms. Taylor:

  Dear Mr. Alvarez:

- To set off an important idea.

  Directions: Read each sentence and find the adverb.

  Use a semicolon for the following:

- Between independent clauses not joined by coordinate conjunctions (*and*, *but*, *or*, or *nor*.)

  Tonya wanted to go to the movies; Deidre wanted to go shopping.

- Between independent clauses when the second clause begins with words such as *however*, *for instance*, *for example*, *thus*, *furthermore*, *nevertheless*, *therefore*, and *as a result*.

  We arrived at the airport in plenty of time; however, our flight didn't leave for several hours.

- Between independent clauses if there are commas in one or both of the clauses.

  Amy excels at softball, basketball, and track; but her sister is an outstanding singer, dancer, and violinist.

- Between items in a series if the items contain commas.

  For our science project, our group had to find, focus, and research a topic; make charts, tables, and models; and give an oral presentation to the class.

8.7 Name Change

Fort Dearborn was one of the first names for the site that became this major American city. What city was built on this site?

To answer the question, read each sentence below. Determine whether the colons and semicolons are used correctly. If the sentence is correct, write the letter for "correct" in the space above the sentence number at the bottom of the page. If a colon or semicolon is missing, or is used incorrectly, write the letter for "incorrect." You will need to reverse the letters.

1. As the early settlers moved westward from the original thirteen colonies, they experienced many hardships: however, the promise of a new life drew them forward.

   N. Correct   I. Incorrect

2. The government encouraged westward expansion; as a result, pioneers by the thousands headed to the frontier.

   A. Correct   U. Incorrect

3. Daniel Boone was a frontiersman; he led settlers: to Kentucky.

   V. Correct   C. Incorrect

4. In history; Amy is studying about the pioneers.

   D. Correct   C. Incorrect

5. History is her first class in the morning at 8:30: and she enjoys this class.

   S. Correct   G. Incorrect

6. In her opinion, it is amazing how the pioneers survived the following hardships: severe storms, drought, lack of food, and attacks by Native Americans.

   H. Correct   E. Incorrect

7. The pioneers kept moving westward; they conquered the frontier.

   O. Correct   R. Incorrect

___ ___ ___ ___ ___ ___ ___
7   5   2   3   1   6   4

Punctuation and Capitalization

Apostrophes

Apostrophes are used to show the possessive case of nouns and to indicate omitted letters in contractions.

- Show the possessive case of singular nouns by adding an apostrophe and *-s*.

  Examples: Lila's cell phone, the kitten's toy mouse, James's bike, the baby's crib, the tree's roots, the house's roof

  An exception to this rule is for nouns of more than one syllable that end in an *-s* sound. The singular possessive case may be formed by adding only an apostrophe.

  Examples: Moses' beliefs, the witness' explanation, Mr. Rogers' sweater

- Show the possessive case of plural nouns that end in *-s* by adding an apostrophe.

  Examples: the two brothers' business, the horses' stable, the girls' soccer team

- Show the possessive case of plural nouns that do not end in *-s* by adding an apostrophe and *-s*.

  Examples: a men's clothing store, the children's tickets, the geese's nesting grounds

- Use an apostrophe to indicate missing letters in a contraction.

I am	I'm
can not	can't
do not	don't
could have	could've
they are	they're
that is	that's
you will	you'll
it is	it's

8.8 Independence

This colony was the first to declare independence from England, six months before the signing of the Declaration of Independence. Which colony was this?

To answer the question, match the words on the left with their correct form on the right. Choose your answers according to the specific form called for in the parentheses after the word. Write the letter of each answer in the space above its number at the bottom of the page. You will need to reverse the letters and divide them into words.

1. brother (plural possessive)	A. brothers'	I. brother's
2. sister (singular possessive)	N. sisters'	S. sister's
3. child (plural possessive)	U. childrens'	I. children's
4. kitten (singular possessive)	M. kitten's	G. kittens'
5. city (plural possessive)	R. cities'	S. cities's
6. car (singular possessive)	O. cars'	W. car's
7. puppy (plural possessive)	P. puppies'	I. puppie's
8. we have (contraction)	N. we've	S. we'ave
9. can not (contraction)	J. cann't	E. can't
10. they are (contraction)	H. they're	A. the're

___ ___ ___ ___ ___ ___ ___ ___ ___ ___ ___ ___
 9   5   3   10   2   7   4   1   10   6   9   8

8.9 Famous Battle

This was the first major armed conflict between American and British troops in what was to become the Revolutionary War. Where did this conflict occur?

To answer the question, read each sentence below. If the apostrophes are used correctly, write the letter for "correct" in the space above the sentence number at the bottom of the page. If at least one apostrophe is used incorrectly or is missing, write the letter for "incorrect." You will need to reverse the letters.

1. The Revolutionary War was fought between the colonies' and England.
   A. Correct   N. Incorrect

2. Many colonists' loyalty to the Crown was strong, and they didn't support the war.
   O. Correct   E. Incorrect

3. The king's advisors didn't understand the colonists' deep resentment of Parliament's laws.
   G. Correct   R. Incorrect

4. "No taxation without representation" became the colonists' rallying cry.
   T. Correct   N. Incorrect

5. Many American's hoped the problem wouldn't lead to war.
   A. Correct   N. Incorrect

6. But in many people's opinions war was inevitable.
   I. Correct   L. Incorrect

7. Relations between the colonists' and England were poor for several years.
   H. Correct   E. Incorrect

8. No one could've predicted how King Georges actions could push the colonies to fight.
   P. Correct   L. Incorrect

9. After several years' of anger toward England, by April of 1775 war couldn't be avoided any longer.
   I. Correct   X. Incorrect

___ ___ ___ ___ ___ ___ ___ ___ ___
 5   2   4   3   1   6   9   7   8

8.10 By Another Name

Before Tennessee became a state in 1796, a part of it was organized as a separate state with another name. What was this "state" called?

To answer the question, read the paragraph below and determine whether each underlined apostrophe is used correctly. Starting with the first sentence, write the letters beneath the correctly used apostrophes in order on the blanks at the bottom of the page.

Kristen, Sues' best friend, is an expert on the states'. Sue is certain that there
         C   H

isn't anything Kristen does not know about the states. For instance, she knows all the
  F

states' capitals, their biggest cities', and their populations. She also knows each state's
  R   E   A

most important industries and tourist sites'. Kristen's favorite state, of course, is
                             U   N

Tennessee. That's because she was born there. In Kristens' opinion, Tennessee's natural
           K   E   L

beauty makes it a wonderful place to live. Sue couldn't agree more with her best
                                       I

friends' opinion, because Sue's home is there, too.
  S   N

___ ___ ___ ___ ___ ___ ___ ___

Punctuation and Capitalization

Quotation Marks

Quotation marks are used to set off the words of speakers and to indicate certain titles.

- Use quotation marks to set off the direct words of a speaker. A direct quote begins with a capital letter. It is separated from the rest of the sentence by a comma, unless the quotation ends with a question mark or exclamation point. Commas and end marks are placed inside quotation marks.

  "It is a pleasant day," said Jan.

  Antoine said, "The movie begins at eight."

  "When is the science report due?" asked Will.

- A divided quotation occurs when a speaker tag (for example, *he said*) divides a quotation into two parts. If the second part of the quotation is part of the first, a comma follows the speaker tag and the second part begins with a small letter. If the second part of the quotation starts a new sentence, it must begin with a capital letter.

  "If it is nice Saturday," said Allie, "we can go hiking."

  "It is supposed to be nice Saturday," said Allie. "We can go hiking."

- Use single quotation marks to indicate a quotation within a quotation.

  "Tom said, 'The game is at home,'" said Lisa.

- Use quotation marks to indicate certain titles, including stories, songs, articles, chapters of books, and poems.

  Story: "Raymond's Run"

  Song: "America the Beautiful"

  Article: "How to Earn Great Grades"

  Chapter of Book: "The Best Part-Time Jobs for Kids"

  Poem: "The Raven"

8.11 Icy Fog

This heavy winter fog contains ice crystals. It occurs mostly in the mountain valleys of the western United States. What is it called?

To answer the question, read each sentence below. If the quotation marks and punctuation with them are used correctly, write the letter after the sentence in the space above the sentence number at the bottom of the page. If the quotation marks or the punctuation with them is incorrect, <u>do</u> <u>not</u> write any letter in the space. When you are done, cross out the empty blanks. The letters that remain will be your answer.

1. Last night Marvin watched a TV special titled "Our Changing Climate." (I)

2. "I agree said Sheila. Yesterday it was supposed to be sunny, but it rained all day." (E)

3. "I think that the weather is hard to predict," said Marvin. (N)

4. "What time was that program on? asked Sheila. (A)

5. "Nine o'clock," Marvin said. "It was a great show." (G)

6. "I'm sorry I missed it." Sheila said. (Y)

7. Marvin said, "I really learned a lot from the program." (O)

8. "Maybe someday you'll be a meteorologist," Sheila said. (P)

9. "Who knows," said Marvin. "maybe I will." (D)

___ ___ ___ ___ ___ ___ ___ ___ ___ ___ ___
 8   2   7   4   5   7   6   3   1   8   9

Punctuation and Capitalization

8.12 Women and Voting

This country was the first to give women the right to vote, in 1893. What country was this?

To answer the question, read each sentence below. If the quotation marks and the punctuation with them are correct, write the letter for "correct" in the space above the sentence number at the bottom of the page. If the quotation marks or the punctuation with them is incorrect, write the letter for "incorrect." You will need to divide the letters into words.

1. "Susan B. Anthony was a leader in the struggle to gain the right for women to vote," said Ashley.

   L. Correct   M. Incorrect

2. "The right to vote is called suffrage." said Taylor.

   A. Correct   Z. Incorrect

3. "I did a report on Susan B. Anthony," said Marla. "She was a remarkable woman."

   N. Correct   E. Incorrect

4. "Her fight for women's rights began in 1851," Marla said, "When she met Elizabeth Cady Stanton."

   E. Correct   W. Incorrect

5. "Who was she?" asked Taylor.

   D. Correct   N. Incorrect

6. "I've heard of her," said Ashley. "She was a leader in the women's rights movement."

   N. Correct   G. Incorrect

7. Marla said "Stanton and Anthony worked together for a constitutional amendment giving women the right to vote."

   R. Correct   E. Incorrect

8. "The United States was not the first country to give women the right to vote, said Ashley."

   U. Correct   A. Incorrect

___ ___ ___ ___ ___ ___ ___ ___ ___ ___
 6   7   4   2   7   8   1   8   3   5

8.13 New World Explorer

This man was the first European explorer to find Manhattan Island. Who was he?

   To answer the question, read each sentence below. If the quotation marks and the punctuation with them are correct, write the letter for "correct" in the space above the sentence number at the bottom of the page. If the quotation marks or the punctuation with them is incorrect, write the letter for "incorrect." You will need to divide the letters into words.

1. "I think we should do our project on explorers." Roxanne said to her friend Stephanie.
   N. Correct   S. Incorrect

2. "OK, but which ones," said Stephanie.
   N. Correct   R. Incorrect

3. "How about European explorers of the 'New World'?" said Roxanne.
   Z. Correct   U. Incorrect

4. She opened a book to Chapter 10, "New World Explorers."
   E. Correct   A. Incorrect

5. "This will get us started," she said, "but we'll need more information.
   S. Correct   O. Incorrect

6. "I'll check the Internet," Stephanie said. "There should be plenty of helpful sites."
   N. Correct   R. Incorrect

7. "Should we begin with Columbus?" Stephanie asked.
   D. Correct   A. Incorrect

8. "Let's find the explorers we feel are most interesting," said Roxanne, "and narrow it down from there."
   Y. Correct   A. Incorrect

9. "We'd better start," said Stephanie, "Because we have a lot to do."
   V. Correct   H. Incorrect

___ ___ ___ ___ ___ ___ ___ ___ ___ ___ ___
 9   4   6   2   8   9   3   7   1   5   6

Italics

. . . .

Italics are used to show certain titles and names. They are letters that lean to the right in printed material. In handwritten material, underlining is used in place of italics.

Use italics (or underlining) to show the following:

- The titles of books, plays, movies, and TV shows.

  Book: *Sing Down the Moon*

  Play: *Julius Caesar*

  Movie: *The Incredibles*

  TV Show: *Jeopardy*

- The names of newspapers and magazines.

  Newspaper: *The New York Times*

  Magazine: *Discover*

- The names of ships, trains, planes, and spacecraft.

  Ship: *Titanic*

  Train: *Orient Express*

  Plane: *Air Force One*

  Spacecraft: *Voyager*

- Works of art.

  Painting: *Mona Lisa*

  Sculpture: *Gamin*

- Words for emphasis.

  It's and *its* do not mean the same thing.

. . . .

8.14 Born at Sea

This was the first child born on the *Mayflower* during its voyage to the New World. What was this child's name?

To answer the question, decide whether the names and titles below require italics. If a name or title is correctly written in italics, write the letter for "correct" in the space above its number at the bottom of the page. If a name or title is incorrect, write the letter for "incorrect."

1. *Main Street*
   R. Correct   A. Incorrect

2. the *New York Yankees*
   E. Correct   I. Incorrect

3. the starship *Enterprise*
   U. Correct   S. Incorrect

4. the poem *The Raven*
   H. Correct   C. Incorrect

5. the novel *The Outsiders*
   S. Correct   E. Incorrect

6. the train *Cannonball Express*
   K. Correct   V. Incorrect

7. *Dallas, Texas*
   Y. Correct   H. Incorrect

8. the magazine *National Geographic*
   E. Correct   A. Incorrect

9. the *Star-Spangled Banner*
   C. Correct   O. Incorrect

10. the newspaper *Los Angeles Times*
    P. Correct   A. Incorrect

11. the TV show *The Simpsons*
    N. Correct   L. Incorrect

___ ___ ___ ___ ___ ___ ___   ___ ___ ___ ___ ___ ___ ___
 9   4   8   1   11   3   5   7   9   10   6   2   11   5

Punctuation and Capitalization

8.15 Moonless Planets

These two planets in our solar system do not have any moons. Which planets are they?

To answer the question, read each sentence below. If the underlined words or titles should be italicized, write the letter for "italics" in the space above the sentence number at the bottom of the page. If the underlined words or titles should not be italicized, write the letter for "no italics." You will need to divide the letters into words.

1. For her <u>birthday</u>, Jill's Uncle Ted gave her a new telescope.
   U. Italics   N. No italics

2. He also gave her a book titled <u>Our Solar System</u>.
   C. Italics   N. No italics

3. Jill has always been interested in <u>astronomy</u>.
   P. Italics   Y. No italics

4. She imagines what it must have been like to be an astronaut on <u>Apollo 11</u> and land on the moon.
   S. Italics   O. No italics

5. Science fiction movies such as <u>Star Wars</u> are among her favorite movies.
   M. Italics   H. No italics

6. Jill is interested in other <u>science subjects</u>, too.
   M. Italics   V. No italics

7. She likes the magazine <u>Discover</u>, because it has articles on many topics in science.
   U. Italics   T. No italics

8. But space and our <u>solar system</u> fascinate her.
   A. Italics   R. No italics

9. <u>War of the Worlds</u> is one of her favorite novels.
   E. Italics   R. No italics

___ ___ ___ ___ ___ ___ ___ ___ ___ ___ ___ ___
 5   9   8   2   7   8   3   6   9   1   7   4

8.16 Bird-Eating Bug

Hummingbirds are so small that one of their predators is an insect. What insect preys on hummingbirds?

To answer the question, determine whether each name or title on the left requires quotation marks or italics. Choose your answers from the column labeled "Quotation Marks" or the column labeled "Italics." Write the letter of each answer in the space above its number at the bottom of the page. You will need to divide the letters into words.

	Quotation Marks	Italics
1. King Kong (movie)	R	M
2. The Open Window (short story)	S	N
3. Yankee Doodle (song)	R	C
4. All About Dogs (book)	W	G
5. Caring for Your Puppy (book chapter)	T	L
6. The Phantom of the Opera (play)	R	Y
7. The Secret Garden (novel)	S	P
8. The Road Not Taken (poem)	N	U
9. The Scout (painting)	P	I
10. Santa Maria (ship)	O	A

___ ___ ___ ___ ___ ___ ___ ___ ___ ___ ___ ___ ___
 7   3   10   6   9   8   4   1   10   8   5   9   2

8.17 One of the First Systems of Writing

The Sumerians were a people of the ancient Middle East. About fifty-five hundred years ago they invented a system of writing that used symbols to represent words. What was this system of writing called?

To answer the question, read each sentence below. Decide whether the underlined word or words require quotation marks, italics, or neither. Write the letter of each answer in the space above its sentence number at the bottom of the page.

1. Veronica read a book about <u>ancient history.</u>
   U. Quotation marks   L. Italics   I. Neither

2. In Chapter 4, <u>The Sumerians</u>, she learned about a people who lived over five thousand years ago.
   O. Quotation marks   U. Italics   E. Neither

3. They lived in a land called <u>Mesopotamia.</u>
   A. Quotation marks   T. Italics   E. Neither

4. Veronica learned more about these people in a book titled <u>Ancient Lands and Peoples.</u>
   I. Quotation marks   U. Italics   S. Neither

5. Her friend Gianna asked, <u>What did you learn?</u>
   R. Quotation marks   E. Italics   U. Neither

6. Veronica explained that Mesopotamia was home to many <u>early civilizations.</u>
   P. Quotation marks   H. Italics   C. Neither

7. Veronica looked for articles about Mesopotamia in the magazine <u>National Geographic.</u>
   I. Quotation marks   M. Italics   C. Neither

8. Gianna suggested that Veronica watch a TV special titled <u>Lost Lands.</u>
   C. Quotation marks   N. Italics   L. Neither

9. <u>I'll check the Internet, too,</u> said Veronica.
   F. Quotation marks   M. Italics   R. Neither

___ ___ ___ ___ ___ ___ ___ ___ ___
 6   4   8   3   1   9   2   5   7

8.18 Side by Side

Most animals walk by moving alternating legs. Only three animals walk by moving the legs on one side of their body, then moving the legs on the other side. Two of these animals are the cat and the camel. What is the third?

To answer the question, read each sentence below. If the quotation marks and italics are used correctly, write the letter for "correct" in the space above the sentence number at the bottom of the page. If either quotation marks or italics are used incorrectly, write the letter for "incorrect."

1. Chapter 8, "Unusual Mammals," was the most interesting chapter in the book titled *Mammals*.
   A. Correct   J. Incorrect

2. "According to a recent *TV program*," said Amy, "mammals are found throughout the world."
   A. Correct   E. Incorrect

3. "They are the dominant species on our planet, said Josh."
   A. Correct   I. Incorrect

4. "In the magazine called *Discover*, I read that blue whales are the biggest mammals," said Amy.
   F. Correct   I. Incorrect

5. "I read an article titled *Little Mammals*," said Amy, "and learned that some of the smallest mammals are bats."
   U. Correct   R. Incorrect

6. "Have you ever read the poem "A Bat Is Born"?" said Josh.
   U. Correct   F. Incorrect

7. "If you are interested in mammals," said Amy, "you might enjoy checking websites on the Internet."
   G. Correct   J. Incorrect

—	—	—	—	—	—	—
7	3	5	1	6	4	2

Punctuation and Capitalization

8.19 Nation's Capital

Washington, D.C., our nation's capital, was not always named Washington. What was its original name?

To answer the question, match the phrase describing the *use* of the punctuation mark on the left with its punctuation mark on the right. Write the letter of each answer in the space above the phrase's number at the bottom of the page. One punctuation mark will be used more than once. You will need to divide the letters into words.

1. Shows a speaker's exact words

2. Sets off a list

3. Indicates a title of a book

4. Ends a statement

5. Shows ownership

6. Separates items in a series

7. Ends a sentence of strong emotion

8. Indicates italics in handwritten material

9. Ends an interrogative sentence

10. Ends a command or order

11. Connects two independent clauses not joined by a conjunction

E. Period

C. Question mark

D. Exclamation point

T. Comma

R. Colon

F. Semicolon

A. Quotation marks

I. Italics

L. Apostrophe

Y. Underlining

___ ___ ___ ___ ___ ___ ___ ___ ___ ___ ___
11   4   7   10   2   1   5   9   3   6   8

8.20 Keeping Warm

In 1873, Chester Greenwood of Maine invented a popular item for keeping warm. What did he invent?

To answer the question, read each sentence below and identify the missing punctuation mark. Choose your answers from the punctuation marks that follow each sentence. Write the letter of each answer in the space above its sentence number at the bottom of the page.

1. The average persons normal body temperature is 98.6 degrees.
    W. Comma   I. Period   U. Apostrophe

2. When Leah caught a cold last week she had a fever.
    A. Comma   E. Period   H. Apostrophe

3. Her temperature rose to 102 degrees and she felt miserable.
    S. Comma   N. Period   D. Apostrophe

4. Fortunately, she recovered from her cold in a few days
    D. Comma   F. Period   E. Apostrophe

5. She was glad to get back to school she had a lot to do.
    T. Comma   M. Semicolon   D. Colon

6. "How are you feeling" said Mrs. Williams, her science teacher.
    O. Comma   N. Period   R. Question mark

7. "I'm fine," Leah said "but I'm a little tired."
    E. Comma   H. Period   W. Apostrophe

8. Leah made the following list of all her makeup work math, reading, social studies, and English.
    E. Comma   R. Semicolon   F. Colon

___ ___ ___ ___ ___ ___ ___ ___
 7   2   6   5   1   8   4   3

8.21 A Lot of Water

In Alaska, vast amounts of frozen water are contained in more than a hundred thousand of these. What are they?

To answer the question, read each sentence below and identify the missing punctuation mark. Choose your answers from the punctuation marks that follow the sentences. Write the letter of each answer in the space above its sentence number at the bottom of the page. Not all answers will be used.

1. Alaska, the biggest state in our country is also the northernmost and certainly among the coldest.

2. Mike is moving to Alaska he expects to leave next week.

3. Mike has several reasons for moving to Alaska, including the following the state's natural beauty, its wilderness areas, and its rugged environment.

4. Mikes Uncle Todd and his family have lived in Alaska for many years.

5. Last year Mike read about Alaska in an article titled "Wilderness Lands.

6. "When will you be coming" said Uncle Todd.

7. "My flight arrives next Tuesday at 3:45 PM. in Anchorage," said Mike.

8. During the flight Mike read Alaska, a magazine containing articles about the state.

Answers

L. Quotation marks   R. Question mark   E. Comma   I. Colon   C. Italics
U. Exclamation point   S. Apostrophe   A. Semicolon   G. Period

___ ___ ___ ___ ___ ___ ___ ___
7   5   2   8   3   1   6   4

8.22 Tornado State

On average, this state has more tornadoes than any other. What state is this?
   To answer the question, read each sentence below and identify the missing punctuation mark. Choose your answers from the punctuation marks that follow the sentences. Write the letter of each answer in the space above its sentence number at the bottom of the page. Not all answers will be used.

1. When Hallie was studying tornadoes in science she was surprised to learn that more tornadoes occur in the United States than in any other country.

2. "Did you know that the winds of a tornado can be as high as 300 miles per hour? said Jenna, her friend.

3. Hallie looked in Chapter 10, "Violent Storms," in her science book for more information

4. "I checked this book out of the library," said Jenna, handing Hallie a book titled Tornado Alley.

5. "Theres incredible information in this book," she said.

6. "Does it explain what causes tornadoes" said Hallie.

7. Hallie was most interested in the causes of tornadoes Jenna was most interested in how they could be predicted.

8. When class ended at 240, the girls went to the library to find more information.

Answers

O. Quotation marks   K. Question mark   A. Period   M. Colon   L. Italics

W. Exclamation point   O. Semicolon   H. Apostrophe   A. Comma

___ ___ ___ ___ ___ ___ ___ ___
 7   6   4   1   5   2   8   3

8.23 Theodore Roosevelt

Punctuation and Capitalization

According to some accounts, this favorite toy was named after Theodore Roosevelt. What was the toy?

   To answer the question, read each sentence below and identify the missing punctuation mark. Choose your answers from the punctuation marks that follow the sentences. Write the letter of each answer in the space above its sentence number at the bottom of the page. If no punctuation marks are missing, write the letter for "None." Not all answers will be used. You will need to divide the letters into words.

1. Mrs. Thompson's class was learning about Theodore Roosevelt the twenty-sixth president of the United States.

2. She explained that Roosevelt was vice president to William McKinley however, when McKinley was assassinated in 1901, Roosevelt assumed the presidency.

3. When he assumed office, Roosevelt was the youngest man to serve as president.

4. "Roosevelt was one of the most popular US. presidents," said Mrs. Thompson.

5. "Was he a hero in the Spanish-American War" Mrs. Thompson asked.

6. "Roosevelts interest in the environment resulted in setting aside 125 million acres as national forests," she said.

7. "For homework, she said, "read Chapter 7 in your text."

8. "For more information about Theodore Roosevelt," Mrs. Thompson said, "you should consult the book titled Theodore Roosevelt: His Life and Times."

Answers

R. Period   T. Question mark   A. Comma   M. Colon   D. Italics

Y. None   E. Quotation marks   B. Apostrophe   S. Semicolon

___ ___ ___ ___ ___ ___ ___ ___ ___ ___
 5   7   8   8   3   6   7   1   4   2

8.24 Big Trees

Capable of growing up to three hundred feet, this tree is considered to be one of the world's biggest. What is it?

To answer the question, read the paragraph below. Find each incorrectly used punctuation mark. Starting with the first sentence, write the letters beneath the incorrectly used punctuation marks in order on the blanks at the bottom of the page.

Scientists estimate that the Earth is home to between sixty thousand, and seventy
S

thousand species of trees. Some scientists wonder if there are even more than
G

seventy thousand? Except in extremely dry or cold regions, trees are found
E   R

throughout the world. Trees may be grouped into two broad categories; evergreen
M   Q

trees and deciduous trees. Evergreen trees, such as pines, and spruces, keep their
I   T   U   T

leaves through the year. Deciduous trees, such as maples and oaks, lose their leaves'
A   R   B   O

as cold weather approaches. Did you know that much of the world's oxygen comes
H   U

from trees. Trees absorb carbon dioxide from the air, and they release oxygen as a
I   W

by-product: of photosynthesis. Photosynthesis, of course, is the process by which
A   K   E   N

green plants use light to turn water and carbon dioxide into food.
S

___ ___ ___ ___ ___ ___ ___

Punctuation and Capitalization

8.25 Voyage to the New World

The Pilgrims sailed from England to the New World on a surprisingly small ship. In terms of size, what would their ship be about equal to today?

To answer the question, read each sentence below. If all the punctuation is correct, write the letter for "correct" in the space above the sentence number at the bottom of the page. If any of the punctuation is incorrect or is missing, write the letter for "incorrect." You will need to divide the letters into words.

1. The Pilgrims left England on September 16 1620.
   E. Correct   O. Incorrect

2. They sailed on the Mayflower.
   G. Correct   I. Incorrect

3. On November 21, the ship dropped anchor in a sheltered harbor.
   R. Correct   E. Incorrect

4. On that same day, the men wrote and signed a constitution.
   E. Correct   B. Incorrect

5. Called the Mayflower Compact, this was the "first constitution" written in the New World.
   O. Correct   C. Incorrect

6. The Pilgrims went on to found the Plymouth Colony.
   S. Correct   M. Incorrect

7. This was the first permanent English settlement in New England.
   U. Correct   I. Incorrect

8. It was not the first English settlement in the New World, that distinction went to Jamestown in Virginia.
   I. Correct   N. Incorrect

9. The *Jamestown Colony* was founded on May 14, 1607.
   A. Correct   T. Incorrect

___ ___ ___ ___ ___ ___ ___ ___ ___ ___ ___
 9   4   8   8   2   6   5   1   7   3   9

8.26 Great Buy

In 1867, the United States purchased Alaska from Russia for $7,200,000. This was certainly one of the best real estate purchases of all time. What was the approximate cost for each acre of Alaskan land?

To answer the question, read each sentence below. If all the punctuation is correct, write the letter for "correct" in the space above the sentence number at the bottom of the page. If any of the punctuation is incorrect or is missing, write the letter for "incorrect." You will need to divide the letters into words.

1. Alaska became the forty-ninth state of the Union on Jan 3, 1959.
   U. Correct   C. Incorrect

2. Alaska, sometimes called the Final Frontier, is admired for its rugged environment and vast size.
   T. Correct   D. Incorrect

3. Alaska is rich in natural resources, and wildlife.
   S. Correct   O. Incorrect

4. Until 1867; Alaska belonged to Russia.
   O. Correct   T. Incorrect

5. "Secretary of State" William H. Seward negotiated the purchase of Alaska by the United States from Russia.
   N. Correct   S. Incorrect

6. In many people's opinions back then, Alaska was a cold wasteland.
   N. Correct   A. Incorrect

7. They called the purchase Sewards Folly.
   H. Correct   W. Incorrect

8. These people couldn't have been more wrong.
   E. Correct   S. Incorrect

___ ___ ___ ___ ___ ___ ___ ___
 4   7   3   1   8   6   2   5

8.27 Oceania

Most geography books refer to the thousands of islands in the central and southern Pacific as Oceania. In the past, these islands were often referred to by another name that occasionally is still used today. What was that name?

   To answer the question, find the missing or incorrectly used punctuation mark in each sentence below. Select the punctuation mark that corrects the mistake from the choices that follow the sentences. Write the letter of each answer in the space above the sentence number at the bottom of the page. Not all answers will be used. You will need to divide the letters into words.

1. Until she studied Oceania in school: Tia never realized how many islands were located in the Pacific Ocean.

2. "Wow," she said, amazed. "I can't believe how big the Pacific Ocean is."

3. "What are you looking at," said Sharyn.

4. "Oceania, said Tia, studying a map in her textbook.

5. "Isn't the setting of the novel 'Call It Courage' in the Pacific?" said Sharyn.

6. "Yes, it is," said Tia, "That's a great book."

7. "Maybe theres a copy of it in the library," said Sharyn.

Answers

T. Period	O. Question mark	Y. Colon
H. Italics	A. Exclamation point	S. Semicolon
S. Apostrophe	E. Quotation marks	U. Comma

___ ___ ___ ___ ___ ___ ___ ___ ___ ___ ___ ___
6   5   4   7   3   1   6   5   7   4   2   7

8.28 Southern Capital

This state capital is the southernmost in the forty-eight contiguous states. What is it?

To answer the question, find the missing or incorrectly used punctuation mark in each sentence below. Select the punctuation mark that corrects the mistake from the choices that follow the sentences. Write the letter of each answer in the space above the sentence number at the bottom of the page. Not all answers will be used. You will need to divide the letters into words.

1. Jons group was preparing for a class geography bee.

2. "Let's review the state capitals." said Julie. "Does everyone agree?"

3. "OK," said Marc. "What's the capital of Florida."

4. "It's Tallahassee," said Umberto, "Name the capital of Arizona."

5. "I think it's Phoenix," said Julie, but let me check."

6. She opened a book titled "States of the Union" and turned to Chapter 4, "States and Their Capitals."

7. Jon continued to ask questions: the others continued to answer them.

8. "The geography bee begins at 115," said Jon.

Answers

N. Period   U. Question mark   A. Colon

X. Italics   Y. Exclamation point   S. Semicolon

I. Apostrophe   T. Quotation marks   E. Comma

___ ___ ___ ___ ___ ___ ___ ___ ___ ___ ___
 8   3   7   5   1   4   5   2   6   8   7

Punctuation and Capitalization

Capitalization

Always capitalize the following:

- The pronoun "I."

- Proper nouns.

  Examples: Abraham Lincoln, Maya Angelou, Golden Gate Bridge

- Proper adjectives.

  Examples: American culture, Mexican food, the German people

- Initials.

  Examples: John F. Kennedy, J. K. Rowling, E. B. White

- Titles when they come before a name.

  Examples: Doctor Jones, Captain Smith, Officer Ortiz, Aunt Alice, Minister Hart

- The days of the week and the months of the year.

  Examples: Sunday, Tuesday, January, November

- The names of cities, states, countries, and continents.

  Examples: Chicago, Texas, United States of America, Africa

- The names of rivers, lakes, oceans, mountains, and other geographical sites.

  Examples: Amazon River, Lake Superior, Pacific Ocean, Mount Everest, Rocky Mountains, Sahara Desert, Grand Canyon, North Pole

- The names of streets and avenues.

  Examples: Main Street, Lakeview Boulevard, River Avenue, Hillside Road

- The names of public and religious holidays.

  Examples: Fourth of July, Christmas, Yom Kippur, Ramadan

- The names of companies, organizations, agencies, and clubs.

  Examples: Ford Motor Company, Federal Bureau of Investigation, the Smithton Better Business Bureau, the Pleasantville Ice Skating Association

Capitalization (continued)
. . . .

- The names of important historical documents and events.

  Examples: Declaration of Independence, American Revolution, Civil War

- The first word in a sentence.

  Rain fell heavily through the night.

- The first word in a quotation.

  Taryn said, "The report is due on Friday."

- The first word, last word, and all important words in the titles of books, poems, songs, movies, TV shows, plays, and works of art.

  Book: *The Slave Dancer*

  Poem: "The Road Not Taken"

  Song: "America the Beautiful"

  Movie: *Finding Nemo*

  Sculpture: *The Harp*

- All of the words of the greeting of a letter. Capitalize only the first word of the closing of a letter.

  Dear Mr. Timmons,

  Sincerely yours,

  Yours very truly,

- Most abbreviations.

  Examples: Mr., Mrs., Dr., Ave., Tues., Dec.

8.29 Low-Lying Land

With about 40 percent of its land below sea level, this country is the lowest country in the world. What is it?

To answer the question, identify the correct capitalization for each item below. Write the letter of each answer in the space above its number at the bottom of the page.

1. mr. harris, the mayor
   Z. Mr. Harris, the Mayor   H. Mr. Harris, the mayor

2. dr. shannon a. willis
   L. Dr. Shannon a. Willis   R. Dr. Shannon A. Willis

3. 5 river road
   S. 5 River Road   Y. 5 River road

4. aunt barbara
   W. aunt Barbara   T. Aunt Barbara

5. call of the wild (novel)
   A. *Call of the Wild*   U. *Call Of The Wild*

6. washington monument
   D. Washington Monument   E. Washington monument

7. captain williams
   H. captain Williams   L. Captain Williams

8. columbia river
   R. Columbia river   E. Columbia River

9. "studying for tests" (article)
   N. "Studying for Tests"   G. "Studying for tests"

___ ___ ___ ___ ___ ___ ___ ___ ___ ___ ___
 9   8   4   1   8   2   7   5   9   6   3

8.30 Heading West!

Because it served as a starting point for wagon trains heading west, St. Louis gained a special nickname. What was this name?

To answer the question, determine which letter in each of the following is incorrect. This letter may be a letter that needs to be capitalized, or it may be a letter that is capitalized but should not be. Find this letter among the answers that follow. Write its corresponding letter (in the parentheses) in the space above the item number at the bottom of the page. If all of the letters are correct, write the letter for correct. Not all answers will be used. You will need to divide the letters into words.

1. Paul A. Simmons, jr.

2. Sara's Sister

3. Rio Grande river

4. Museum of natural History

5. the United Nations

6. pastor Martin

7. North America, a Continent

8. ms. Francis Smith

9. Great Salt lake

Answers

N (S)	G (N)	J (H)	P (A)	S (O)	C (E)
L (T)	R (Y)	M (G)	A (R)	Correct (W)	

— — — — — — — — — — — — — — — —
8 6 9 7 5 6 3 9 2 9 1 7 5 7 4 9

Punctuation and Capitalization

8.31 Country with Many Islands

With over 81,000 islands, this country is thought to possess more islands than any other country in the world. What is it?

To answer the question, read each sentence below. If all of the capital letters are correct, write the letter for "correct" in the space above the sentence number at the bottom of the page. If at least one letter that should be capitalized is not capitalized, or if a letter that should not be capitalized is, write the letter for "incorrect."

1. Many nations throughout the World are made up partly of islands.
   H. Correct   N. Incorrect

2. Located in the Pacific Ocean, the country of Indonesia consists of nearly fourteen thousand islands.
   A. Correct   L. Incorrect

3. Indonesia stretches some thirty-two hundred miles across the Sea.
   U. Correct   L. Incorrect

4. Numerous other island nations are located throughout the Pacific.
   N. Correct   E. Incorrect

5. The atlantic Ocean is home to island nations, too.
   I. Correct   D. Incorrect

6. The United Kingdom is an island nation off the Coast of France.
   A. Correct   I. Incorrect

7. Although some island nations are made up of thousands of islands, the nation with the most islands is a part of Europe.
   F. Correct   H. Incorrect

```
__   __   __   __   __   __   __
 7    6    1    3    2    4    5
```

Punctuation and Capitalization

8.32 L. M. Montgomery

L. M. Montgomery was the author of *Anne of Green Gables*. What do the initials L. M. stand for?

To answer the question, read each sentence below. If all of the capital letters are correct, write the letter for "correct" in the space above the sentence number at the bottom of the page. If at least one letter that should be capitalized is not capitalized, or if a letter that should not be capitalized is, write the letter for "incorrect." The first letter is provided. You will need to divide the letters into words.

1. Recently some of the students of ms. Larsen's class were discussing books.
   R. Correct   U. Incorrect

2. "My favorite book of all time," said Tina, "Is *Charlotte's Web*."
   A. Correct   C. Incorrect

3. "Mine is *A Wizard of Earthsea*," said Albert. "It's a great book."
   A. Correct   E. Incorrect

4. "Was the author of that book Ursula k. LeGuin?" asked Robin.
   K. Correct   D. Incorrect

5. "Yes," said Albert. "I enjoy her stories, especially the parts with magic."
   U. Correct   A. Incorrect

6. "Me, too," said Charles, "but my favorite story is *Lord Of The Rings*."
   A. Correct   Y. Incorrect

7. "All of you are mentioning great books," said Cheryl. "As for me, I love *Anne of Green Gables*."
   M. Correct   P. Incorrect

L   __ __ __ __ __ __ __
    5   2   6   7   3   1   4

8.33 Icy City

This Russian city is the largest city north of the Arctic Circle. What is its name?

To answer the question, read each sentence below. Find the incorrect letter. This letter may be a letter that needs to be capitalized, or it may be a letter that is capitalized but should not be. Write the letter in the space above its sentence number at the bottom of the page.

1. Winters in the Area north of the Arctic Circle are cold and long.

2. A surprising number of plants and animals live in this cold Region of the world.

3. More than four hundred Species of flowering plants bloom during the Arctic's short summers.

4. Numerous mammals and birds live in the Arctic, but few live near the north Pole.

5. Except for Alaska, no state in the united States extends north of the Arctic Circle.

6. Robert Peary and his assistant matthew A. Henson led an expedition to the North Pole in 1909.

7. One of the Keys to Peary's successful expedition was his great determination.

```
 __   __   __   __   __   __   __   __
 6    5    2    6    1    4    3    7
```

Punctuation and Capitalization

8.34 Spinning Straw into Gold

In one of the fairy tales of the Brothers Grimm, this dwarf could spin straw into gold. Who was he?

To answer the question, decide which of the following pairs is written with correct capitalization. Write the letter of each answer in the space above its number at the bottom of the page.

1. E. Mediterranean Sea   S. the Roman empire

2. K. Grand Canyon   U. Jefferson ave.

3. R. Great plains   U. Museum of Natural History

4. I. Gulf Of Mexico   L. Western Hemisphere

5. Z. Ocean currents   N. Rocky Mountains

6. M. nations of Europe   A. new Hampshire

7. J. fluffy, our pet cat   S. Orlando, Florida

8. E. monday, Oct. 12th   I. J. K. Rowling

9. P. Joe's Tire Service   M. Mountains of the world

10. R. Dr. Steven Harrison   S. Washington, dc

11. M. san Francisco   T. Mount Rushmore

___ ___ ___ ___ ___ ___ ___ ___ ___ ___ ___ ___ ___ ___ ___
10   3   6   9   1   4   7   11   8   4   11   7   2   8   5

Punctuation and Capitalization

Usage and Proofreading

Word usage is an important part of grammar. Just about every English and language arts teacher has seen students mix up words like *affect* and *effect*, *good* and *well*, and *lay* and *lie* more times than they would ever care to recall. Even when students understand the meanings of these words, they may make mistakes with them if they are not careful. Because these words, and words like them, are easily confused, they often slip into speaking and writing unnoticed. Students can avoid making usage mistakes by understanding the meanings of easily confused words and proofreading their written work with care and concentration.

The tip sheets and worksheets that follow focus on word usage and proofreading. The first tip sheet identifies several of the most easily confused words in English, and Worksheets 9.1 through 9.6 provide students with practice in recognizing and using these words correctly. The second tip sheet offers students guidelines for proofreading for mistakes in grammar, and Worksheets 9.7 through 9.14 focus on proofreading practice, also providing a general review of grammar.

Confusing Words

Several words in English are so easily confused that they result in numerous mistakes for speakers and writers. The following list contains some of the most common and confusing of these words.

- accept–except

  accept (verb): to receive or to agree to

  except (preposition): excluding or but

- affect–effect

  affect (verb): to influence

  effect (noun): result

  effect (verb): to bring about

- all ready–already

  all ready (adjective): completely prepared

  already (adverb): by this time

- all together–altogether

  all together (pronoun; adjective): everything or everyone in a place

  altogether (adverb): entirely

- bad–badly

  bad (adjective): can be used only to modify a noun or pronoun

  badly (adverb): can be used to modify verbs, adjectives, or other adverbs

- breath–breathe

  breath (noun): air inhaled and exhaled during respiration

  breathe (verb): to inhale and exhale air

- conscience–conscious

  conscience (noun): a sense of right and wrong

  conscious (adjective): aware

Confusing Words (continued)

- council–counsel

  council (noun): an official group

  counsel (verb): to offer advice

  counsel (noun): advice

- desert–dessert

  desert (noun): very dry land

  dessert (noun): food served at the end of a meal

- device–devise

  device (noun): something constructed

  devise (verb): to plan

- envelop–envelope

  envelop (verb): to wrap or enclose

  envelope (noun): a covering for a letter

- farther–further

  farther (adjective): to a greater distance in terms of length or space

  further (adjective): beyond a certain point in terms of time, degree, or quantity

- formally–formerly

  formally (adverb): in accordance with the rules

  formerly (adverb): previously

- good–well

  good (adjective): can be used only to modify a noun or pronoun

- well (adverb): can be used to modify verbs, adjectives, or other adverbs

  well (adjective): used to refer to health

(continued)

Confusing Words (continued)

- in–into

   in (preposition): inside or within

   into (preposition): implies movement toward the inside

- its–it's

   its (pronoun): possessive form of *it*

   it's (contraction): *it is*

- later–latter

   later (adjective): past the expected time

   latter (adjective): the second of two

- lay–lie

   lay (verb): to set or place something down

   lie (verb): to recline or to rest

- loose–lose

   loose (adjective): not tight

   lose (verb): misplace; not win

- personal–personnel

   personal (adjective): private

   personnel (noun): people who work in the same place

- picture–pitcher

   picture (noun): a drawing or photograph

   pitcher (noun): a container for holding a liquid; a baseball player

- quiet–quit–quite

   quiet (adjective): little or no noise

   quit (verb): to stop

   quite (adverb): very

Confusing Words (continued)

- than–then

  than (conjunction): used to make comparisons

  then (adverb): at a particular time; next in order of time

- their–there–they're

  their (pronoun): possessive case of *they*

  there (adverb): in, at, or near a particular place

  they're (contraction): *they are*

- threw–through

  threw (verb): past tense of *throw*, meaning to hurl through the air

  through (preposition): going into one side and out the other

- who–whom

  who (pronoun): which or what person

  whom (pronoun): the objective case of *who*

- whose–who's

  whose (pronoun): possessive case of *who*

  who's (contraction): *who is*

- your–you're

  your (pronoun): possessive case of *you*

  you're (contraction): *you are*

9.1 Flying Across the Atlantic

In 1927, this individual was the first to fly solo nonstop from New York to Paris. What was this person's name?

To answer the question, match each word on the left with its definition on the right. Write the letter of each answer in the space above its number at the bottom of the page. You will need to divide the letters into words.

1. accept	H. to plan
2. conscious	D. leaving out or excluding
3. device	E. contraction for *it is*
4. later	N. very dry land
5. except	R. a sense of right and wrong
6. its	L. food served after a main meal
7. desert	I. to receive or agree to
8. devise	S. occurring after the expected time
9. latter	G. something constructed
10. dessert	A. aware
11. it's	B. the second of two
12. conscience	C. possessive form of *it*

__ __ __ __ __ __ __ __ __ __ __ __ __ __ __ __
6 8 2 12 10 11 4 10 1 7 5 9 11 12 3 8

Usage and Proofreading

9.2 Green Plants

This substance makes the leaves of plants look green. What is it?

To answer the question, match each word on the left with its definition on the right. Write the letter of each answer in the space above its number at the bottom of the page.

1. breath   Y. to a greater distance (length)

2. lay   C. to inhale and exhale air

3. farther   H. at a place

4. their   L. a photograph

5. picture   P. contraction for *they are*

6. further   O. inhaled and exhaled air

7. there   L. possessive form of *they*

8. lie   O. container for holding a liquid

9. pitcher   H. to put something down

10. breathe   R. to a greater degree

11. they're   L. to recline

___ ___ ___ ___ ___ ___ ___ ___ ___ ___ ___
10   7   4   9   6   1   11   2   3   5   8

Usage and Proofreading

9.3 What Am I Now?

Some insects and animals undergo major changes during their life cycles. A frog, for example, changes from a tadpole that breathes with gills to a frog that breathes with lungs. What is this change called?

  To answer the question, match each word on the left with its definition on the right. Write the letter of each answer in the space above its number at the bottom of the page.

1. whose   H. misplace

2. lose   M. earlier, previously

3. formally   O. contraction for *who is*

4. affect   S. by this time

5. all ready   R. possessive case of *who*

6. loose   I. according to the rules

7. effect   P. not tight

8. who's   E. to influence

9. formerly   A. completely prepared

10. already   T. result

| __ | __ | __ | __ | __ | __ | __ | __ | __ | __ | __ | __ | __ |
| 9 | 4 | 7 | 5 | 9 | 8 | 1 | 6 | 2 | 8 | 10 | 3 | 10 |

9.4 Sunny City

With an average of 332 days of sunshine each year, this city is considered to be one of the sunniest, if not the sunniest, in the United States. What is this city's name, and in what state is it located?

To answer the question, match each word on the left with its definition on the right. Write the letter of each answer in the space above its number at the bottom of the page. You will need to divide the letters into words.

1. all together   U. within

2. envelop   Y. people who work in the same place

3. in   R. absence of noise

4. personal   A. to enclose

5. quiet   Z. very

6. altogether   A. to stop

7. into   N. a covering for a letter

8. quit   O. private

9. envelope   A. entirely

10. personnel   M. movement toward the inside

11. quite   I. everyone in the same place

___ ___ ___ ___ ___ ___ ___ ___ ___ ___ ___
10   3   7   2   8   5   1   11   4   9   6

Usage and Proofreading

9.5 Yerba Buena

Yerba Buena was the name of this city (although at the time it was not big enough to be a city) until 1847. What modern city was once called Yerba Buena?

   To answer the question, complete each sentence below. Choose your answers from the words that follow each sentence. Write the letter of each answer in the space above its sentence number at the bottom of the page. You will need to divide the letters into words.

1. "I like learning about American history," said James. "_____ my favorite topic in history class."
   E. Its   I. It's

2. "What is _____ favorite topic?" he asked.
   R. your   O. you're

3. "_____ not going to believe this," said Salvatore, "but I like the Revolutionary War."
   S. Your   N. You're

4. "I like learning about the Founding Fathers," he said. "_____ some of the most interesting people in history."
   H. Their   S. They're   C. There

5. "_____ the most important in your opinion?" said James.
   S. Whose   O. Who's

6. "I can't decide _____ achievements were the greatest," said Salvatore.
   F. whose   I. who's

7. "_____ are so many leaders who had a great impact on our country," said James.
   O. Their   U. They're   A. There

8. "_____ lives were fascinating," said Salvatore.
   C. Their   N. They're   L. There

___ ___ ___ ___ ___ ___ ___ ___ ___ ___ ___ ___
 4   7   3   6   2   7   3   8   1   4   8   5

Usage and Proofreading

© Gary Robert Muschla

9.6 Key to Ancient Writing

This slab of rock with writing dates back to 196 B.C. It enabled scholars to decipher ancient Egyptian hieroglyphics. What is the name of this rock?

   To answer the question, complete each sentence below. Choose your answers from the words that follow each sentence. Write the letter of each answer in the space above its sentence number at the bottom of the page. You will need to divide the letters into words.

1. Archaeologists are men and women _____ study past civilizations.
   I. whom   A. who

2. They _____ the challenge of unlocking the secrets of history.
   R. accept   E. except

3. Many of ancient Egypt's secrets are hidden in the _____.
   N. desert   E. dessert

4. _____ are many secrets to find.
   L. They're   N. Their   E. There

5. Archaeologists spend much of _____ time trying to understand the past.
   L. they're   S. their   I. there

6. Ancient Egyptian hieroglyphics was a type of _____ writing.
   E. pitcher   O. picture

7. Life today is very different _____ it was in ancient times.
   E. than   U. then

8. The _____ archaeologists look into the past, the more secrets they will unlock.
   C. farther   T. further

   __ __ __ __ __ __ __ __ __ __ __ __
   2   6   5   4   8   8   1   5   8   6   3   7

Usage and Proofreading

Proofreading for Mistakes in Grammar

When you are proofreading to find mistakes in grammar, follow the basic guidelines described here.

1. The first word in a sentence, all proper nouns, the pronoun *I*, and all proper adjectives are capitalized.

2. All sentences have correct ending punctuation: periods for declarative and imperative sentences, question marks for interrogative sentences, and exclamation points for exclamatory sentences.

3. Commas are used to separate items in a list; to set off introductory words, phrases, and clauses; between city and state; in dates; after direct address; and to set off quotations.

4. Apostrophes are used to show possessive nouns and to indicate contractions.

5. Colons are used for time and to set off lists.

6. Semicolons are used to join independent clauses when a conjunction is not used, and to join items in series that already contain commas.

7. Quotation marks are used for the titles of stories, songs, poems, the chapters of books, and to show the direct words of speakers.

8. Italics are used for the titles of books, plays, TV shows, and movies; for the names of newspapers and magazines; and for the names of certain vehicles.

9. Subjects agree with their verbs.

10. Pronouns agree with their antecedents.

11. The tenses of verbs are correct.

12. All words are used correctly.

Of course, along with proofreading for mistakes in grammar, you should make sure that all spelling is correct. You should also be certain that you have used the best words to share your ideas.

9.7 Giant Lizard

This lizard can grow to be ten feet long and weigh up to 360 pounds. What is the name of this lizard?

To answer the question, read each sentence below and identify the sentence's grammatical mistake. There will be no more than one mistake in each sentence. Select your answers from the choices that follow the sentences. Write the letter of each answer in the space above its sentence number at the bottom of the page. If there are no mistakes, write the letter for "correct." Not all answers will be used.

1. There are about three thousand Species of lizards in the world.

2. Lizards is reptiles that are found mostly in warm climates.

3. Most lizards have a long body a long tail, short legs, and scales.

4. Some lizards were only a few inches long, but others are several feet in length.

5. Unlike mammals, lizards are cold-blooded; their bodies are the same temperature as the air

6. Most lizards are harmless to people, but a few are poisonous.

7. Gila monsters', which are common in New Mexico and Arizona, are poisonous lizards.

8. If you want to learn more about lizards, a good book is Lizards of Planet Earth.

Answers

A. Capitalization	G. Period	S. Question mark
T. Colon	C. Semicolon	D. Apostrophe
O. Italics	K. Verb tense	M. Subject-verb agreement
R. Correct	N. Comma	A. Quotation marks

___ ___ ___ ___ ___ ___   ___ ___ ___ ___ ___ ___
 4   8   2   8   7   8   7   6   1   5   8   3

Usage and Proofreading

9.8 Pseudonym of a Famous Author

This author's real name was Samuel Langhorne Clemens. What was his pseudonym, or pen name?

To answer the question, read each sentence below and identify the sentence's grammatical mistake. There will be no more than one mistake in each sentence. Select your answers from the choices that follow the sentences. Write the letter of each answer in the space above its sentence number at the bottom of the page. If there are no mistakes, write the letter for "correct." Not all answers will be used. You will need to divide the letters into words.

1. Samuel Langhorne Clemens was born on November 30 1835 in Missouri.

2. As a young man, Clemens wrote for the Hannibal Journal, a newspaper owned by his older brother.

3. Later he worked as a printer and a steamboat pilot on the Mississippi river.

4. After the Civil War, Clemens headed: west.

5. He eventually settled in Virginia City, Nevada, and he became a newspaper reporter.

6. I'm not certain if this was where he began signing his articles with a pseudonym

7. The name he chose was a Mississippi phrase from his steamboat days that meant "two fathoms deep.

8. Clemens dies in April of 1910.

Answers

W. Capitalization	N. Period	H. Question mark
T. Colon	U. Semicolon	L. Apostrophe
R. Italics	M. Verb tense	D. Subject-verb agreement
K. Correct	I. Comma	A. Quotation marks

___ ___ ___ ___ ___ ___ ___ ___ ___
 8   7   2   5   4   3   7   1   6

Usage and Proofreading

9.9 Capital of the North

This city is the world's northernmost capital. What is its name?

To answer the question, read each sentence below and identify the sentence's grammatical mistake. There will be no more than one mistake in each sentence. Select your answers from the choices that follow the sentences. Write the letter of each answer in the space above its sentence number at the bottom of the page. If there are no mistakes, write the letter for "correct." Not all answers will be used.

1. Despite its northern location this city has a surprisingly moderate climate.

2. Mild ocean currents that flow northward from the south "influence" the climate.

3. Vikings explored and settled here well over a thousand years ago

4. According to some historians, a norwegian by the name of Arnarson was among the first settlers.

5. Today, this city is the capital of an island nation.

6. Roberta looked up information about this city in an *atlas*.

7. In another book she found that volcanoes and hot springs is located throughout the island.

8. Most buildings are heated by water; that is piped from nearby hot springs.

Answers

Y. Capitalization	I. Period	M. Question mark
S. Colon	J. Semicolon	U. Apostrophe
R. Italics	K. Verb tense	K. Subject-verb agreement
V. Correct	A. Comma	E. Quotation marks

___ ___ ___ ___ ___ ___ ___ ___ ___
6   2   4   7   8   1   5   3   7

Usage and Proofreading

9.10 Ancient Historian

This man is often called the Father of History. Who was he?

To answer the question, read each sentence below and identify the sentence's grammatical mistake. There will be no more than one mistake in each sentence. Select your answers from the choices that follow the sentences. Write the letter of each answer in the space above its sentence number at the bottom of the page. If there are no mistakes, write the letter for "correct." Not all answers will be used.

1. This man was born about 484 B.C. in whats now Turkey.

2. At that time, Turkey was known as persia.

3. Although he is born in Persia, he was Greek.

4. After leaving the land of his birth about 457 B.C., he traveled threw much of the ancient world.

5. He learned much about the customs and history of the people of many lands.

6. He settled in southern Italy about 443 B.C

7. It was here that he began writing a great book, simply titled History.

8. This book deals: with the legends, traditions, and conflicts of the ancient world.

9. Most modern historians "consider this to be the first true" history book.

Answers

R. Capitalization	U. Period	M. Comma
H. Colon	K. Semicolon	T. Apostrophe
O. Quotation marks	O. Italics	D. Verb tense
L. Subject-verb agreement	E. Word usage	S. Correct

___ ___ ___ ___ ___ ___ ___ ___ ___
 8   4   2   9   3   7   1   6   5

9.11 Major Volcanic Eruption

Many scientists believe that the biggest volcanic eruption in modern times occurred on March 6, 1815. What was the name of this volcano?

To answer the question, read each sentence below and identify the sentence's grammatical mistake. There will be no more than one mistake in each sentence. Select your answers from the choices that follow the sentences. Write the letter of each answer in the space above its sentence number at the bottom of the page. If there are no mistakes, write the letter for "correct." Not all answers will be used. You will need to divide the letters into words.

1. The students in Mr. Jamisons science class were studying volcanoes.

2. The students learned that volcanic eruptions is caused by molten rock that rises to the surface of the Earth.

3. Sometimes the molten rock, called magma erupts with great violence.

4. One of the greatest eruptions in modern times occurred in 1815 on the Indonesian island of Sumbawa.

5. So much dust and ash are sent into the sky that the sun's light was dimmed for several months.

6. This triggered a period of: global cooling.

7. The following year came to be known as the 'year without a summer.'

8. That year, summer frost killed crops as far south as Virginia, and snow fell in August in new England.

Answers

O. Capitalization   S. Period   U. Comma

T. Colon   E. Semicolon   B. Apostrophe

C. Italics   N. Verb tense   A. Subject-verb agreement

I. Word usage   R. Correct   M. Quotation marks

___ ___ ___ ___ ___ ___ ___ ___ ___ ___ ___ ___
7   8   3   5   6   6   2   7   1   8   4   2

Usage and Proofreading

9.12 Delightful Idea

In 1904, Italo Marchiony was granted a patent for this delightful way to eat a favorite treat. What was his patent for?

To answer the question, read each sentence below and identify the sentence's grammatical mistake. There will be no more than one mistake in each sentence. Select your answers from the choices that follow the sentences. Write the letter of each answer in the space above its sentence number at the bottom of the page. If there are no mistakes, write the letter for "correct." Not all answers will be used. You will need to divide the letters into words.

1. Natalia was looking forward to her Birthday party.

2. "I can't hardly wait," she said to Jenna and Brittany. "Can you come early to help me set up?"

3. "Sure," said Jenna. "Brit and me will come around six."

4. "Great" said Natalia. "Everything's just about ready."

5. Natalias mother helped her prepare for the party before the other girls arrived.

6. "Do you think everyone will come" said Natalia.

7. It wasn't long before everyone started arriving.

8. Right after everyone sang Happy Birthday to You, Natalia began opening her gifts.

Answers

A. Capitalization	S. Period	M. Question mark
I. Comma	U. Colon	J. Semicolon
N. Apostrophe	C. Quotation marks	W. Italics
O. Double negative	R. Pronoun usage	E. Correct

___ ___ ___ ___ ___ ___ ___ ___ ___ ___ ___ ___
4   8   7   8   3   7   1   6   8   2   5   7

9.13 Important Words

These words are the foundation of all spoken and written English. What are they?

To answer the question, read each sentence below and decide whether the statement is true or false. If it is true, write the letter for "true" in the space above the sentence number at the bottom of the page. If it is false, write the letter for "false." You will need to reverse and divide the letters into words.

1. A verb can only show action.
   C. True   E. False

2. A pronoun is a word that can take the place of a noun or another pronoun.
   U. True   C. False

3. An adjective can modify nouns, pronouns, and other adjectives.
   B. True   N. False

4. Adverbs modify nouns, pronouns, verbs, adjectives, and other adverbs.
   T. True   R. False

5. A preposition is a word that relates a noun or pronoun to another word in a sentence.
   B. True   S. False

6. A noun is a person, place, thing, or idea.
   O. True   A. False

7. A conjunction can join words and phrases, but not clauses.
   J. True   V. False

8. An interjection always stands alone and has no grammatical relationship to other words in a sentence.
   N. True   S. False

___ ___ ___ ___ ___ ___ ___ ___
 5   4   1   7   3   2   6   8

9.14 A Puzzle About You

If you get all of the following right, you will learn something about yourself. What are you?

   To answer the question, read each sentence below and decide whether the statement is true or false. If it is true, write the letter for "true" in the space above the sentence number at the bottom of the page. If it is false, write the letter for "false." You will need to divide the letters into words.

1. There are nine parts of speech in English.
    S. True   I. False

2. A declarative sentence is a statement.
    W. True   D. False

3. An imperative sentence asks a question.
    O. True   E. False

4. A direct object gives action to a verb.
    S. True   H. False

5. An independent clause can stand alone as a sentence.
    R. True   N. False

6. An indirect object can be the subject of a sentence.
    O. True   A. False

7. Subjects must always agree with their verbs in number.
    T. True   D. False

8. Both possessive nouns and possessive pronouns show ownership and require apostrophes.
    T. True   M. False

9. Proper nouns and proper adjectives must be capitalized.
    G. True   A. False

___ ___ ___ ___ ___ ___ ___ ___ ___ ___ ___ ___ ___ ___ ___ ___
 9   5   3   6   7   2   1   7   4   9   5   6   8   8   6   5

Answer Key

The answers for the worksheets contain both the letters of the correct answers for individual items as well as the answers to the questions posed at the beginning of each worksheet. For those activities in which students must read a paragraph as they complete the worksheet, the entire paragraph is reproduced in the answer key, with the correct answers highlighted in bold. For activities in which students must identify a specific word and letter, both the word and letter are included.

Part 1

1.1   1. L 2. S 3. R 4. C 5. Y 6. A 7. T 8. E 9. M
Mary Celeste

1.2   1. N 2. D 3. O 4. R 5. E 6. G 7. P 8. L 9. A
Edgar Allan Poe

1.3   1. U 2. A 3. I 4. C 5. B 6. E 7. L 8. R 9. X
Excalibur

1.4   1. O 2. L 3. H 4. S 5. N 6. T 7. M 8. A 9. I 10. E
The Mona Lisa

1.5   1. U 2. T 3. O 4. E 5. L 6. U 7. E 8. F 9. O 10. S 11. S
Slue-Foot Sue

1.6   1. O 2. R 3. A 4. C 5. E 6. K 7. Y 8. B 9. W 10. J
Jabberwocky

1.7   The answers for the paragraph are marked in bold.
Are you familiar with the midnight ride of Paul Revere? Paul Revere was born in
     B   **T**   **R**
Boston in 1735. A silversmith and engraver by trade, he was a steadfast patriot. With
  D   **N** **O**   **J**
other patriots, Revere took part in the Boston Tea Party of 1773. During the war,
    K **W**   **H**   **C**

Revere carried messages for patriot troops. With two other men, he carried his most
$\overline{\text{N}}$ $\overline{\text{L}}$ $\overline{\text{U}}$ $\overline{\text{B}}$

important message on the night of April 18, 1775. He hoped to warn the patriots of
$\overline{\text{S}}$ $\overline{\text{E}}$ $\overline{\text{V}}$

approaching British troops. In a strange twist of history that night, Revere did not
$\overline{\text{H}}$ $\overline{\text{A}}$

warn the patriots. British scouts stopped and questioned him. Fortunately, one of the
$\overline{\text{U}}$ $\overline{\text{T}}$

other men with Revere was able to slip by the British scouts and warn the patriots. A
$\overline{\text{W}}$

poem, "Paul Revere's Ride," by Henry Wadsworth Longfellow, secured a place in
$\overline{\text{Y}}$

history for Revere.
$\overline{\text{A}}$

Brown Beauty

1.8 1. K 2. E 3. S 4. N 5. I 6. R 7. A 8. L 9. D 10. O
Roanoke Island

1.9 The answers for the paragraph are marked in bold.
Baseball is an American game. Early versions of the game were based on the
$\overline{\text{R}}$ $\overline{\text{B}}$ $\overline{\text{U}}$ $\overline{\text{E}}$

British games of cricket and rounders. Both cricket and rounders are played with teams
$\overline{\text{D}}$ $\overline{\text{C}}$

and bats and a ball. In both games, players score points by passing stations, or bases.
$\overline{\text{S}}$ $\overline{\text{C}}$

By the 1840s, American baseball slowly was taking its modern form. The game grew
$\overline{\text{U}}$ $\overline{\text{T}}$ $\overline{\text{O}}$

in popularity during the 1850s. By the late 1850s several clubs played the game. The
$\overline{\text{N}}$ $\overline{\text{C}}$

first professional baseball team was started in Cincinnati in 1869. Two years later, the first
$\overline{\text{E}}$ $\overline{\text{K}}$

professional baseball association was organized. The National League, still in operation
$\overline{\text{D}}$ $\overline{\text{I}}$ $\overline{\text{M}}$

today, was founded in 1876. Several other associations and leagues followed. Teams in
$\overline{\text{N}}$ $\overline{\text{G}}$ $\overline{\text{H}}$

the American League began playing in 1900. Because of its great popularity, baseball
$\overline{\text{S}}$

has been called the national pastime.
$\overline{\text{D}}$

Red Stockings

1.10 1. O 2. E 3. R 4. U 5. A 6. L 7. S 8. P 9. T
Pluto Platters

1.11 1. S 2. I 3. A 4. U 5. O 6. E 7. F 8. N 9. M
Famous Funnies

1.12 1. N 2. E 3. R 4. T 5. C 6. O 7. I 8. A 9. Y 10. D
Decoration Day

1.13   1. R 2. O 3. G 4. N 5. W 6. A 7. M 8. L 9. I
William Morgan

1.14   1. A 2. K 3. I 4. R 5. E 6. L 7. F 8. B 9. N
Ben Franklin

1.15   1. W 2. L 3. N 4. C 5. E 6. U 7. H 8. O 9. T 10. S
The New Colossus

1.16   1. R 2. U 3. I 4. M 5. L 6. S 7. F 8. O 9. T 10. E
Flittermouse

1.17   1. T 2. V 3. A 4. H 5. E 6. L 7. Y 8. D
Death Valley

1.18   1. O 2. E 3. S 4. N 5. A 6. R 7. H 8. T
The North Star

1.19   1. N 2. L 3. O 4. P 5. Y 6. O 7. M 8. O
Monopoly

1.20   1. U 2. A 3. O 4. N 5. D 6. Y 7. I 8. R 9. H
Harry Houdini

1.21   1. E 2. O 3. M 4. L 5. P 6. S 7. K 8. A 9. J
James Polk (with letters reversed)

Part 2

2.1   1. M 2. O 3. E 4. R 5. A 6. S 7. Y 8. I 9. N 10. H 11. W 12. L
William Henry Harrison

2.2   1. A 2. B 3. E 4. E 5. L 6. H 7. L 8. U 9. W
Blue Whale

2.3   1. S 2. R 3. H 4. G 5. L 6. C 7. E 8. A 9. B
Charles Babbage

2.4   1. N 2. R 3. M 4. D 5. H 6. B 7. E 8. G 9. A 10. X 11. L
Alexander Graham Bell

2.5   1. L 2. S 3. N 4. R 5. E 6. I 7. U 8. D 9. C 10. A
Daedalus and Icarus

2.6   1. A 2. O 3. A 4. H 5. I 6. L 7. M 8. T 9. K 10. C 11. O 12. Y
Oklahoma City

2.7   1. I 2. S 3. L 4. H 5. A 6. R 7. B 8. N 9. T 10. E 11. K
Katherine Lee Bates

2.8 1. A 2. R 3. R 4. D 5. A 6. O 7. A 8. L 9. N 10. L 11. J 12. E
Lara and Jor-El

2.9 1. S, S 2. O, R 3. C, D 4. E, R 5. N, A 6. C, I 7. R, E 8. M, A
American Red Cross (with letters reversed)

2.10 1. E 2. R 3. N 4. S 5. D 6. L 7. P 8. H 9. A
Alan Shepard

2.11 The answers for the paragraph are marked in bold.
Uranus, the <u>seventh</u> planet, was <u>discovered</u> in 1781 beyond the orbit of Saturn.
                 T   W   **H**   **I**

Uranus is <u>about</u> four times as big as <u>Earth</u> and lies about 1.78 billion <u>miles</u> from the sun.
                 O   **L**   **L**

It <u>takes</u> Uranus about 84 <u>years</u> to make a <u>complete</u> trip around the sun. <u>Although</u>
    M   **I**   **A**   **S**

<u>astronomers</u> do not know <u>much</u> about the <u>surface</u> of the <u>planet</u>, they <u>know</u> that its
       A   **D**   **M**   **H**   **T**

<u>atmosphere</u> is made up <u>mostly</u> of hydrogen, <u>helium</u>, and methane. Through a <u>telescope</u>
        E   **H**   **R**   **S**

Uranus <u>appears</u> to be a <u>bluish-green</u> <u>disk</u>, but its <u>color</u> is not <u>due</u> to any plant life or
           U   **G**   **C**   **M H**   **I**

<u>oceans</u>. The average <u>temperature</u> on the planet is −350 degrees Fahrenheit (−214
   E   **L**

degrees Celsius). Uranus is a cold, <u>inhospitable</u> world.
                                         D

William Herschel

2.12 1. E 2. R 3. L 4. K 5. T 6. E 7. A 8. E 9. B 10. C 11. T
Battle Creek

2.13 1. E 2. A 3. P 4. S 5. R 6. U 7. Q 8. D
Quadrupeds

2.14 1. H 2. E 3. S 4. B 5. Y 6. A 7. C 8. T
Casey at the Bat

Part 3

3.1 1. H 2. N 3. R 4. O 5. B 6. C 7. E 8. A 9. I 10. D
Ichabod Crane

3.2 1. I 2. A 3. U 4. P 5. S 6. L 7. R 8. A 9. M 10. S
Marsupials

3.3 1. R (read) 2. A (contain) 3. T (thinks) 4. W (worries) 5. O (considers) 6. C (capture)
7. L (like) 8. B (borrowed) 9. N (finished) 10. E (returned) 11. R (offered)
Robert Lawrence

3.4   1. O (was introduced) 2. B (was born) 3. S (was developing) 4. W (were produced) 5. E (was featured) 6. M (has become) 7. T (has created) 8. A (have starred) 9. I (will be) 10. L (are loved)
Steamboat Willie

3.5   The answers for the paragraph are marked in bold.
There are about forty-two hundred species of mammals. Mammals have become the
                M   P
dominant life forms on Earth. Dogs, cats, horses, dolphins, bats, and humans

are examples of mammals. Unlike other animals, mammals can adapt to different
               O   L
environments. They are found throughout the world in many habitats. From the poles
                     A
to the equator, mammals have populated the world. Mammals share distinct charac-
                          T   N
teristics. The bodies of mammals are covered with hair. Mammals nourish their young
                              Y   S
with milk. Most mammals give birth to live young. One of their most important charac-
                       T
teristics is being warm-blooded. Their bodies are kept at a constant temperature. This
                P   U
helps mammals to live in both cold and warm climates. Because of their unique charac-
                E
teristics, mammals will remain the dominant life forms on our planet.
                           S
Platypus

3.6   1. I 2. A 3. R 4. O 5. N 6. G 7. E 8. P 9. S
Passenger Pigeon

3.7   1. E 2. L 3. I 4. A 5. F 6. L 7. L 8. B 9. F 10. W
Wiffle Ball

3.8   1. U 2. R 3. T 4. N 5. L 6. E 7. H 8. J 9. O
John Luther Jones

3.9   1. R 2. N 3. I 4. A 5. A 6. N 7. M 8. D
Mandarin

3.10   1. N 2. S 3. L 4. E 5. U 6. T 7. H 8. G 9. C 10. A
Last Chance Gulch

3.11   1. A 2. N 3. T 4. L 5. H 6. E 7. I 8. C 9. O
Echolocation

3.12   1. T (report) 2. C (subject) 3. S (research) 4. I (Internet) 5. O (books) 6. H (hours) 7. L (details) 8. Y (summary) 9. G (grade)
Ichthyologists

3.13 1. A 2. R 3. I 4. C 5. E 6. M 7. K 8. M 9. R
Merrimack

3.14 1. B (Roberto) 2. M (him) 3. F (friend) 4. U (instructor) 5. O (Roberto) 6. L (ball) 7. T (student) 8. G (Gil) 9. H (them)
Tom Thumb Golf

3.15 1. H 2. L 3. N 4. S 5. P 6. E 7. D 8. R 9. W 10. I
Windshield Wipers

3.16 1. A 2. S 3. O 4. N 5. J 6. M 7. A 8. H 9. D
John Adams

3.17 1. L 2. T 3. U 4. U 5. S 6. N 7. Y 8. M 9. P 10. O
Mount Olympus

3.18 1. S 2. H 3. W 4. E 5. M 6. T 7. A
James Matthew

3.19 1. A 2. I 3. O 4. S 5. C 6. H 7. E 8. N 9. L 10. T
The Constellations

3.20 1. X 2. N 3. V 4. L 5. L 6. A 7. I 8. O 9. E
Alexei Leonov

3.21 1. A 2. Y 3. Y 4. H 5. R 6. A 7. M 8. S
Mary Hays

3.22 1. A 2. N 3. S 4. H 5. M 6. O 7. L 8. C 9. E 10. E
Chameleons

3.23 1. N 2. I 3. S 4. T 5. I 6. D 7. A 8. G 9. Q 10. U
Giant Squid

3.24 1. N 2. N 3. G 4. J 5. H 6. E 7. O 8. N 9. L
John Glenn

3.25 1. I 2. E 3. S 4. A 5. R 6. L 7. P 8. P 9. C 10. P
Paper Clips

3.26 1. O 2. Y 3. E 4. P 5. I 6. R 7. G 8. H 9. S 10. L
Hieroglyphs

3.27 1. T 2. E 3. C 4. N 5. S 6. U 7. L 8. H 9. V 10. I
Levi Hutchins

3.28 1. S 2. R 3. M 4. O 5. A 6. E 7. D 8. I 9. C
Ice Cream Soda

3.29 1. I 2. W 3. A 4. Y 5. G 6. P 7. P 8. D 9. D
Dippy Dawg

3.30 The answers for the paragraph are marked in bold.

Edward Jenner <u>was</u> a British physician. He <u>was born on</u> May 17, 1749. Always
S   I

curious about nature, he <u>became a keen</u> observer of the world. This trait <u>would help</u> him
N   F   M

in his research. In Jenner's time, doctors <u>had</u> few medicines <u>for treating</u> serious diseases.
A   T

Many of these diseases <u>resulted</u> in death. After studying medicine for <u>several</u> years,
L   U

Jenner <u>started</u> a medical practice. Hoping <u>to prevent</u> one of the most serious diseases of
L   E

his day, he <u>developed</u> procedures for vaccinating people. His methods <u>were</u> successful.
P   O

Jenner <u>did not fully</u> understand his discovery. About seventy-five years later, the French
R

chemist Louis Pasteur <u>would use</u> Jenner's early work as a basis for his own experiments
X

with vaccines. Today, vaccines <u>protect us</u> from many serious diseases.
M

Smallpox

3.31 1. E 2. A 3. N 4. M 5. T 6. I 7. H 8. D 9. O 10. S
Thomas Edison

3.32 1. A 2. O 3. C 4. T 5. N 6. B 7. M 8. L
Mont Blanc

Part 4

4.1 1. H 2. T 3. L 4. G 5. A 6. R 7. P 8. E 9. O 10. N
Pronghorn Antelope

4.2 1. E 2. I 3. H 4. E 5. R 6. D 7. A 8. S 9. C 10. M
Archimedes

4.3 1. N 2. U 3. A 4. L 5. P 6. O 7. I 8. J 9. H 10. S
John Philip Sousa

4.4 1. H (children) 2. I (finger) 3. T (mother) 4. O (Robbie) 5. J (Jenna) 6. R (sister)
7. P (Pixie) 8. E (Cutie) 9. L (poodle) 10. S (members)
Joseph Lister

4.5 The answers for the paragraph are marked in bold.

Amy, Melissa, and William met in <u>their</u> school's library. <u>They</u> were working
G   D

together on a science project. After the librarian gave <u>them</u> some reference books, the
R

students started searching for possible ideas.

"We need a good topic," Amy said to her friends.
　　E　　　　　　　　　　　　　　A

They began to brainstorm, but couldn't decide on a subject.
　A

"Can you look in here?" said Melissa to William, handing him a book.
　　D　　　　　　　　　　　　　　　　　　　　　　　R

"How about the water cycle?" he said.
　　　　　　　　　　　　　　　S

"That topic sounds good to me," said Amy.
　　　　　　　　　　　N

"There should be enough information for us," said Melissa.
　　　　　　　　　　　　　　　　　　　T

"Who wants to check for information on the Internet?" said Amy.
　E

"I will," said Melissa, giving them a big smile.
Ā　　　　　　　　　　　N

The students began their research.
　　　　　　　　　R

Dead Sea

4.6　The answers for the paragraph are marked in bold.
Kerrie and her older sister Samantha went on a nature walk recently. They took
　　　　　S　　　　　　　　　　　　　　　　　　　　　　　　　　　N

lunch and plenty of equipment with them.
　　　　　　　　　　　　　　H

Do you think we will see any animals?" Kerrie asked as they stood in a small
　O　　　　N　　　　　　　　　　　　　　　　　U

clearing.

"We might," said Samantha. "Please hand me the binoculars."
　S　　　　　　　　　　　　　　　C

Kerrie pulled the binoculars from her knapsack and handed them to her. She
　　　　　　　　　　　　　　　M　　　　　　　　I　　A

watched as Samantha scanned the surrounding area.

"There. Do you see it?" Samantha said, pointing at a stand of trees. "A fawn.
　　　　N　　R

And there's a bigger deer just behind him."
　　　　　　　　　　　　　　T

"Yes," said Kerrie. "I see them. But they don't see us."
　　　　　　　　　Ō　S　L　　Ō

Ostrich (with letters reversed)

4.7　1. I 2. M 3. S 4. I 5. A 6. P 7. B 8. H 9. A 10. N
Amphibians

4.8　1. A 2. O 3. R 4. T 5. F 6. G 7. E 8. H 9. I 10. C
The Chicago Fire

4.9　1. L 2. T 3. O 4. H 5. A 6. K 7. E 8. N
Joanne Kathleen

4.10 1. E 2. T 3. H 4. G 5. P 6. A 7. C 8. B
Cabbage Patch (with letters reversed)

4.11 1. I 2. A 3. R 4. E 5. U 6. L 7. D 8. Q 9. Y 10. C
Quadricycle

4.12 1. E 2. U 3. O 4. L 5. R 6. X 7. T 8. T 9. B
Box Turtle

4.13 1. T 2. N 3. S 4. W 5. O 6. E 7. Y 8. L
Yellowstone (with letters reversed)

4.14 1. U 2. O 3. S 4. L 5. S 6. M 7. M 8. P 9. O 10. N 11. Y
Olympus Mons

4.15 1. I 2. T 3. L 4. S 5. O 6. A 7. N 8. E 9. J 10. M 11. P
James Plimpton

4.16 1. I 2. H 3. E 4. Y 5. S 6. F 7. J 8. L
Jellyfish

4.17 1. I 2. E 3. I 4. S 5. R 6. D 7. L 8. P 9. S 10. K
Spider Silk

4.18 1. N 2. B 3. D 4. A 5. I 6. L 7. E 8. S
Edible Sea Snail

4.19 1. O 2. E 3. N 4. D 5. U 6. R 7. Y 8. H 9. G
Greyhound (with letters reversed)

Part 5

5.1 1. E 2. O 3. A 4. T 5. R 6. N 7. H 8. L 9. S 10. C
Charleston

5.2 1. I 2. H 3. L 4. W 5. S 6. R 7. E 8. F
Ferris Wheel

5.3 The answers for the paragraph are marked in bold.
Tina and her little brother Travis planned a big surprise party for their mother's
____R____ ____L____ ____I__T____ ____C____
birthday. On the day of the party, while their father took their mother shopping, Tina and
____H____ __J__ ____S____
Travis decorated the family room. They hung colorful streamers up and set the table with
____I____ __B__
paper plates. Travis filled plastic cups with cold punch. Their grandmother soon arrived
____A____ __R__ T
with a huge cake. After several guests came, everyone waited for Tina's father to bring
____E__ M ____D__ I

her unsuspecting <u>mother</u> home. When Tina heard the car pull <u>into</u> the driveway, she
     <u>L</u>   V   H

L V ... **H**

turned out the lights. The crowded room was silent. As her mother stepped into the
S **E** **M** **U**

dark room, a happy Tina flipped on the switch. Everyone yelled, "Surprise!"
O **N** **D**

Lithiated Lemon

5.4   1. T (Egyptian) 2. N (Italian) 3. E (Chinese) 4. I (Swedish) 5. A (Mexican)
6. D (England) 7. H (Irish) 8. G (Norwegian) 9. D (Finland) 10. R (Switzerland)
11. H (French)
Right Handed

5.5   1. R (better) 2. M (grimmest) 3. E (worse) 4. A (least) 5. H (rough) 6. W (narrow)
7. Y (hungry) 8. I (thirstier) 9. V (lovely) 10. L (wilder)
William Harvey

5.6   1. C 2. S 3. P 4. D 5. L 6. M 7. A 8. E
Deep Sea Clam

5.7   1. A 2. R 3. N 4. U 5. B 6. P 7. E 8. T
Peanut Butter

5.8   1. O 2. T 3. S 4. L 5. E 6. C 7. E 8. P 9. E
Telescope

5.9   1. R (crude) 2. S (several) 3. M (primitive) 4. T (great) 5. O (long) 6. N (new)
7. A (major) 8. G (significant) 9. E (amateur)
George Eastman

5.10   1. E 2. A 3. M 4. N 5. E 6. G 7. D 8. Y
Ganymede

Part 6

6.1   1. E 2. U 3. N 4. O 5. A 6. R 7. Y 8. L 9. F 10. T
Fauntleroy

6.2   1. E 2. N 3. M 4. I 5. R 6. A 7. D 8. G
Dreaming

6.3   The answers for the paragraph are marked in bold.
To <u>most</u> people, snakes are <u>extremely</u> <u>frightening</u> creatures. Although some
P **A** **R**

snakes are <u>poisonous</u>, most are <u>completely</u> harmless to people. In fact, <u>many</u> snakes are
Y **N** **T** **I**

very beneficial. They eat <u>small</u> animals and rodents, <u>effectively</u> keeping the <u>populations</u>
A **H** **C** **S**

of these animals in check. But this fact is seldom enough to make people think favorably
‾‾‾‾   ‾‾‾‾   ‾‾‾‾‾‾   ‾‾‾‾‾‾‾‾
 E   T L   O   N

of snakes. Suddenly seeing a snake slither across the ground is often a startling
          ‾‾‾‾‾‾‾‾ ‾‾‾‾‾‾   ‾‾‾‾‾‾   ‾‾‾‾‾ ‾‾‾‾‾‾‾‾
            D   K   H   A   I

experience for most of us.
                ‾‾‾‾
                  N

Anaconda

6.4 1. I 2. S 3. E 4. U 5. P 6. K 7. R 8. D 9. M 10. P
Mudskipper

6.5 1. M 2. R 3. A 4. B 5. U 6. S 7. C 8. E
Sea Cucumber

6.6 1. R 2. A 3. A 4. R 5. D 6. K 7. A 8. V
Aardvark

6.7 1. O 2. S 3. C 4. T 5. K 6. E 7. P 8. R
Pet Rocks

6.8 1. D 2. R 3. L 4. H 5. S 6. O 7. E 8. T
Three-Toed Sloth

6.9 1. L (lately) 2. E (clearly) 3. S (soon) 4. B (terribly) 5. U (particularly) 6. I (quickly)
7. O (often) 8. R (eagerly) 9. A (greatly)
Aurora Borealis

6.10 1. C (most completely) 2. S (best) 3. N (more silently) 4. A (most safely) 5. M (more
keenly) 6. O (worst) 7. R (more) 8. F (more often) 9. I (earliest)
Francis Marion

6.11 1. N 2. E 3. L 4. K 5. S 6. M 7. O 8. A
Alaskan Moose

Part 7

7.1 1. L 2. N 3. V 4. P 5. C 6. I 7. R 8. S 9. T 10. A 11. E
Travel in Space

7.2 The answers for the paragraph are marked in bold.
Megan has always been interested in the weather. One of her goals is to become a
            ‾‾‾‾‾‾   ‾‾‾‾   ‾
              S   M   A   F

meteorologist someday. She is fascinated with storms and the movement of weather
                                           ‾‾‾‾   ‾‾‾   ‾‾
                                             E   U   R

systems. She is also concerned about global warming. She thinks global warming will
                ‾‾‾‾   ‾‾‾‾‾
                  A   T

one day change the climate all over the Earth. Megan is a keen observer of the weather.
‾‾‾   ‾‾‾ ‾‾‾‾   ‾‾‾‾   ‾‾
 M   H   S   L   T

She studies weather maps and predicts what the weather will be for her town. Some of her predictions are very accurate.

I   U   E   J

her predictions are very accurate.

S

Jet Stream (with letters reversed)

7.3   1. R (into three parts) 2. U (to a computer) 3. B (of the brain) 4. D (during sleep) 5. I (of this organ) 6. N (in the cerebrum) 7. H (of the body) 8. E (by the medulla) 9. L (for a long time) 10. O (in the coming years)
One Hundred Billion

7.4   1. A 2. N 3. O 4. K 5. I 6. J 7. K 8. U
Kinkajou

7.5   1. N 2. A 3. R 4. H 5. O 6. T 7. S 8. E
Eratosthenes

7.6   1. A 2. R 3. E 4. N 5. S 6. O 7. T 8. D
Tornadoes (with letters reversed)

7.7   1. N (by the moon) 2. O (of the oceans) 3. D (around the world) 4. B (between high and low tide) 5. U (during low tide) 6. F (by the falling and rising water) 7. A (of old sailing vessels) 8. Y (of today)
Bay of Fundy

7.8   1. A 2. O 3. E 4. I 5. T 6. U 7. R 8. N 9. M 10 R 11. N 12. I
Mount Rainier

7.9   1. S 2. I 3. R 4. U 5. H 6. U 7. L 8. O
Urushiol

7.10   1. F (good grief) 2. I (yikes) 3. N (oh, no) 4. E (hey) 5. H (phew) 6. O (oops) 7. T (great) 8. A (ah) 9. R (hooray)
Rotation of Earth

7.11   1. U 2. E 3. A 4. N 5. P 6. I 7. N 8. G
A Penguin

7.12   1. T 2. L 3. R 4. S 5. E 6. K 7. G 8. A
Great Lakes (with letters reversed)

7.13   1. I 2. S 3. I 4. S 5. P 6. I 7. R 8. I 9. I 10. E 11. S 12. S 13. R 14. P 15. M 16. V
Mississippi River

7.14   1. N 2. U 3. T 4. I 5. S 6. A 7. M
Tsunami

Part 8

8.1 1. A 2. I 3. R 4. R 5. N 6. L 7. O 8. G 9. F 10. C 11. P 12. E
Peregrine Falcon

8.2 1. P (place) 2. E (avenue) 3. N (captain) 4. E (Wednesday) 5. R (November) 6. R (Saturday) 7. N (governor) 8. P (September) 9. K (parkway) 10. O (October) 11. F (February) 12. A (boulevard) 13. S (Thursday)
Frank Epperson

8.3 1. I 2. E 3. S 4. A 5. N 6. C 7. R 8. T
Arctic Terns

8.4 1. O 2. I 3. W 4. R 5. T 6. L 7. F 8. E
Eiffel Tower (with letters reversed)

8.5 1. T 2. N 3. S 4. U 5. A 6. I 7. L 8. B
Istanbul

8.6 1. A 2. N 3. D 4. N 5. R 6. L 7. E 8. G
Greenland (with letters reversed)

8.7 1. I 2. A 3. C 4. C 5. G 6. H 7. O
Chicago (with letters reversed)

8.8 1. A 2. S 3. I 4. M 5. R 6. W 7. P 8. N 9. E 10. H
New Hampshire (with letters reversed)

8.9 1. N 2. O 3. G 4. T 5. N 6. I 7. E 8. L 9. X
Lexington (with letters reversed)

8.10 The answers for the paragraph are marked in bold.
Kristen, Sues' best friend, is an expert on the states'. Sue is certain that there
        Č   Ḣ
isn't anything Kristen does not know about the states. For instance, she knows all the
  Ḟ
states' capitals, their biggest cities', and their populations. She also knows each state's
   Ṛ   **Ė**   **Ȧ**
most important industries and tourist sites'. Kristen's favorite state, of course, is
                                U̇   **Ṅ**
Tennessee. That's because she was born there. In Kristens' opinion, Tennessee's natural
         K̇   **Ė**   **L̇**
beauty makes it a wonderful place to live. Sue couldn't agree more with her best friends'
                                       Ī   **S̄**
opinion, because Sue's home is there, too.
        Ṅ

Franklin

8.11 1. I 2. – 3. N 4. – 5. G 6. – 7. O 8. P 9. –
Pogonip (the letters for numbers 2, 4, 6, and 9 should not be used)

8.12 1. L 2. Z 3. N 4. W 5. D 6. N 7. E 8. A
New Zealand

8.13 1. S 2. R 3. U 4. E 5. O 6. N 7. D 8. Y 9. H
Henry Hudson

8.14 1. A 2. I 3. U 4. C 5. S 6. K 7. H 8. E 9. O 10. P 11. N
Oceanus Hopkins

8.15 1. N 2. C 3. Y 4. S 5. M 6. V 7. U 8. R 9. E
Mercury, Venus

8.16 1. M 2. S 3. R 4. G 5. T 6. Y 7. P 8. N 9. I 10. A
Praying Mantis

8.17 1. I 2. O 3. E 4. U 5. R 6. C 7. M 8. N 9. F
Cuneiform

8.18 1. A 2. E 3. I 4. F 5. R 6. F 7. G
Giraffe

8.19 1. A 2. R 3. I 4. E 5. L 6. T 7. D 8. Y 9. C 10. E 11. F
Federal City

8.20 1. U 2. A 3. S 4. F 5. M 6. R 7. E 8. F
Earmuffs

8.21 1. E 2. A 3. I 4. S 5. L 6. R 7. G 8. C
Glaciers

8.22 1. A 2. O 3. A 4. L 5. H 6. K 7. O 8. M
Oklahoma

8.23 1. A 2. S 3. Y 4. R 5. T 6. B 7. E 8. D
Teddy Bears

8.24 The answers for the paragraph are marked in bold.
Scientists estimate that the Earth is home to between sixty thousand, and seventy
                                                                    Ṡ
thousand species of trees. Some scientists wonder whether there are even more than
                                                Ḡ
seventy thousand? Except in extremely dry or cold regions, trees are found throughout
                  Ē   Ṟ
the world. Trees may be grouped into two broad categories; evergreen trees and deciduous
            Ṃ   Q̣
trees. Evergreen trees, such as pines, and spruces, keep their leaves through the year.
      Ī   Ṫ   Ṳ   Ṫ   Ā
Deciduous trees, such as maples and oaks, lose their leaves' as cold weather approaches.
                  Ṟ   Ḅ   Ō   H̱
Did you know that much of the world's oxygen comes from trees. Trees absorb carbon
                                    Ṳ   Ị